T0018221

CONSTANT CHRISTIANITY

Jenny Sidri

iUniverse, Inc.
New York   Bloomington

Constant Christianity

iUniverse books may be ordered through booksellers or by contacting:

iUniverse
1663 Liberty Drive
Bloomington, IN 47403
www.iuniverse.com
1-800-Authors (1-800-288-4677)

ISBN: 978-1-4502-1814-6 (sc)
ISBN: 978-1-4502-1815-3 (ebook)

Library of Congress Control Number: 2010905160

Printed in the United States of America

iUniverse rev. date: 05/18/2010

Scripture taken from the New King James Version®
Copyright © 1982 by Thomas Nelson, Inc. Used by permission. All rights reserved.

Contents

The Ten Commandments
(Catholic Version)

1. I am the Lord your God. You shall have no other gods before Me.
2. You shall not take the name of the Lord your God in vain.
3. Remember the Sabbath day, to keep it holy.
4. Honor your father and your mother.
5. You shall not murder.
6. You shall not commit adultery.
7. You shall not steal.
8. You shall not bear false witness against your neighbor.
9. You shall not covet your neighbor's wife.
10. You shall not covet your neighbor's goods.

Exodus 20:2–17

The Ten Commandments
(Protestant Version)

1. You shall have no other gods but me.
2. You shall not make unto you any graven images.
3. You shall not take the name of the Lord your God in vain.
4. You shall remember the Sabbath and keep it holy.
5. Honor your father and your mother.
6. You shall not murder.
7. You shall not commit adultery.
8. You shall not steal.
9. You shall not bear false witness.
10. You shall not covet anything that belongs to your neighbor.

Exodus 20:2–17

The Two Great
Commandments of Jesus

You shall love the Lord your God with all your heart,
with all your soul, and with all your mind.
This is the first and great commandment.
And the second is like it:
You shall love your neighbor as yourself.
On these two commandments
hang all the Law and the Prophets.

Matthew 22:37–40

Introduction

This handbook is for those who seek good emotions in daily living. It offers practical ways to improve our lives—quietly, peacefully—along life's daily path. I have lived these practical methods and can attest to their credibility. These methods were taught to me by a psychologist, a college professor who also served as a motivational consultant; for forty years he was my mentor. He is now deceased. He and his wife, a physician, received the coveted San Sebastian Medal awarded by Spain in recognition of their outstanding contributions to motivational psychology in the 1950s and 1960s. Methods my mentor taught me are presented in this book, along with my personal research and life experiences. The methods presented here can be applied to those seeking health and a sense of well-being.

My bulimic and anorexic condition caused me to lead a life of self-deceit and self-loathing for many years, while trying to appear normal to others. The signs of irrational eating emerged in my childhood; I thought nothing of eating dozens of saltine crackers with butter and jam or several bowls of ice cream at one sitting. My behavior brought only occasional comments from adults. Only in college did I begin to wonder about my "inability" to restrain myself from the package of bran muffins sitting on my dormitory windowsill. Later on, when I served in the U.S. Army, my eating worsened dramatically, to the extent of hiding in a latrine to regurgitate the just-consumed multiple pieces of blueberry pie. My secret "monster-eating" was revealed when medical professionals sought the source of my unhealthy thinness, and I was promptly assigned to a psychiatrist and internal medicine physician. But it was my mentor, whom I'd known since my early teens, who provided the needed guidance and brought me through the darkest hours to new life. I owe him my life. My desire to share the pathway of continuing recovery spurs the writing of this book. Its contents offer a three-step method for finding daily purpose. Perhaps others can benefit from applying these steps to their own lives.

> *Enter by the narrow gate;*
> *For wide is the gate and broad is the way*
> *that leads to destruction,*
> *And there are many who go in by it.*
> *Because narrow is the gate*
> *And difficult is the way which leads to life,*
> *And there are few who find it.*
>
> *Matthew 7:13–14*

Striving to improve ourselves daily, particularly our characters, leads to the narrow gate. What is the aim? Jesus's words provide the standard: "Therefore you shall be perfect, just as your Father in heaven is perfect" (Matt. 5:48).

"Perfect? Impossible!" some would thunder mockingly. Sarah did too, but hers was an unbelieving laugh upon hearing the angel's prediction that she, at the age of ninety, would bear a son to her husband Abraham, who was one hundred years old. Yet "with God all things are possible" (Mark 10:27), and indeed, Sarah's arms cradled the infant Isaac a year later. Why would Jesus direct us to be perfect if he did not mean for us to reach for it? Excuses for not following the Savior's words may camouflage doubt or fear of change. Yet the Master always means what he says. And his parting directives included, "If you love Me, keep My commandments" (John 14:15). Self-improvement is for everyone—age nine, nineteen, or ninety. We start in the here and now, just as we are, in the ultimate and infinite quest of self-perfection.

"But," others protest, "perfection is unattainable, especially in a limited life span!" Yet life is eternal. We simply begin the journey of self-perfection in this temporal body. The first step is practicing daily self-improvement in every area of life. In the Master's words, we who would follow him must take up our crosses daily, our personal crosses of purging ourselves of selfishness. "Let us lay aside every weight, and the sin which so easily ensnares us, and let us run with endurance the race that is set before us" (Heb. 12:1).

Self-improvement is not as unnatural as it might seem. Does not the pianist begin by playing the humble scales? Does not the pharmacist initially learn basic chemistry? In the same way, we begin where we are, balancing all aspects of life, without stress, without self-condemnation. We measure our daily progress by universal principles, not by the standards of any particular age or century, for God's laws are often ignored by a society that rationalizes and justifies its lust and greed for power. Yet honesty and morality still exist. These virtues span all times.

Self-perfection employs these virtues and brings new purpose to life. A listless, bored existence becomes a thing of the past. A tense, harried life fades away, for now we seek values that follow us after the grave: patience, righteousness, purity of conscience, love of truth.

Jesus the Master forged a pathway for the sincere soul seeking Truth. This book presents three steps toward achieving that goal:

1. Daily meditation.
2. Daily self-inventory.
3. Daily training our thoughts to think in constructive ways.

These steps were presented gradually to me by my mentor, Professor Emerson (a pseudonym, for he is deceased and would want to remain anonymous). He first gave me suggestions to repeat to myself to develop the habit of positive thinking. Many of us may have the unconscious habit of mentally criticizing others or of expecting illness or of dreading a certain encounter. Uplifting biblical passages are an excellent countermeasure to such negativism and provide superior mental training. For example, my personal paraphrasing of Ephesians 4:22–23 reads, "I reject the old self and renew my mind in a universal outlook." The next step he gave me was the daily inventory. It focused on balancing all needs of the self (physical, mental, spiritual). Later on, the daily inventory included character perfection as the aim of daily living. For example, in the evening I would sit down and study my behavior that day, asking myself questions such as: *Was I selfish today? Were my emotions in turmoil? Why?* Then the last step was given by my mentor: daily meditation to calm the mind, release tension, and help the meditator evolve into a more compassionate and genuine self. None of these steps is easy. But continuous efforts gradually produce lasting results.

Some might say, "Why bother? Those things take too much time, and I'm content the way I am." We either go forward or go backward in life; we don't stand still. Standing water stagnates; flowing springs become clear. We do change, every moment, because change is part of life.

And while change is part of new scientific knowledge, science now agrees with many of the unchanging biblical precepts:

1. The power of thought (envisioning success brings it)
2. The value of love (compassion generates peace)
3. The need for inner awareness (relaxation reduces stress)

Dr. Hebert Benson, Associate Professor of Medicine at Harvard Medical School and Director of the hypertension section of Boston's Beth Israel Hospital, asserts in his book *The Relaxation Response* that scientific measurements of the human body support "the concept of meditation as a highly relaxed condition associated with lowered activity in a sympathetic nervous system" [1] and that "meditation causes bodily energy resources to be taxed less." [2]

Unchanging biblical concepts and others taught by the Master contribute to a sterling character, and the development of a sterling character affects all aspects of a purposeful and fulfilling life. The only requirements are interest and commitment, for progress takes time. Applying the principles of basic psychology, or common sense, opens the door to our self-perfection.

Many of these psychological principles operate in the world of both mind and matter. For example, Sir Isaac Newton discovered the scientific principle that for every action there is an opposite and equal reaction, as stated in Newton's Third Law of Motion. [3]

A ball thrown against a wall will rebound. This action-reaction reality also operates in man's mental world. Action-reaction of mind is a daily phenomenon. A person who yells angrily at another will generally receive a fury of angry words in return, *unless* the individuals have learned to think before speaking. "A soft answer turns away wrath," advises Proverbs 15:1. If we seek an understanding of human nature, we can rise above negative emotional outbursts, and respond instead with reasoned words based on universal ideals. Maturity may be measured in part by our responses to life. Do we react with reason or with undue emotion stemming from self-centeredness? The small child's self-centered tantrums show the undue emotional response of the untrained soul. The immature adult whose wishes are thwarted and who responds with gossip when not promoted, or curses when he or she does not make the green light, or pouts when the family selects an alternate restaurant, reveals emotions not balanced with reason. Such a soul still focuses on the self as the all-important factor, not the good of the whole or the right course of action. In Genesis 4, we are told that the brothers Cain and Abel both bring offerings to God, but God prefers Abel's offering. Had Cain overcome his uncontrolled passions and used reason, he might have realized his offering to God was not the best or first quality, as was his brother Abel's. When God favored Abel's sacrifice, Cain became jealous, and the Bible's first murder took place. Cain's wounded pride lashed out at his brother, who had only pure intentions. If Cain had wondered *why* his own offering had been rejected, we would have witnessed the Bible's first daily self-study of character.

The ancients say that the practice of *right living* is the highest aim of man. According to Confucius, "The practice of right-living is deemed the highest, the practice of any other art lower. *Complete virtue* takes *first place*; the doing of anything else whatsoever is subordinate" (italics mine).[4] And what is *"right living"*? It is that which brings harmony, not destruction. Some people unconsciously ignore the harmony of the Golden Rule, which tells us to treat others as we want to be treated: "Whatever you want men to do to you, do also to them" (Matt. 7:12). The harmonizing element of the Golden Rule is forgotten whenever people selfishly put themselves first. This can be as simple as jumping line in the school cafeteria. If the schoolboy is not shown the error of his way by parents and teachers, he will jump the line later in life at the local grocery store and ultimately in the corporation, using sophisticated, devious tactics. In daily conversation, we ignore the Golden Rule anytime we inconsiderately interrupt others or fail to respect their points of view.

Why do we commit these infractions in life? Because we have not been shown the value of right living, and thus we remain on the immature level of me-first. Yachts, mink coats, fame, power over others—these never satisfy the deepest longings of the human heart. When the wealthy, famous man finds himself still searching for happiness, he then realizes that something deeper in his nature needs fulfillment. This something is the spiritual element found in every human soul. We can't see it or touch it, and we may even ignore it as we justify our reasons to cheat or lie. Yet many have called for a priest or minister as death approaches. Why do people fail to seek development of their spiritual nature? Because doing so involves facing our character failures—the ones we tend to excuse. People resist change. It's more comfortable and convenient to stay as we are—until we hit rock bottom. At one point in my life, I was parked in a service station parking lot, sobbing, at a loss, and feeling out of control. The warm weather meant the car window was rolled down. Suddenly, in the midst of my sobs, I heard a voice and turned. A young woman with brown hair pulled back from her face leaned down and said gently, "Only you can do it yourself." She turned and returned to a nearby car. I sat, astounded. Who was that? How did she know my state? Yet her words had registered deeply. A quiet determination rose within me. I would fulfill my responsibilities, do my duty, and overcome my immature self-pity. The "woman from nowhere" appeared when I had hit rock bottom. She made me face myself. It's easier to give up than it is to get up. But get up we must.

When the drunkard, glutton, sensualist, or other misguided soul reaches this lowest level and no human agency can help him, he finally turns within, where science cannot reach. When no doctor, no counselor, no psychologist or psychiatrist can help him, then a person falls on his knees and says, "If there is a God, please help me." Then he is willing to think in wider terms and admit his need for help from a Higher Power. Then prayer and meditation become meaningful.

But we do not have to reach such an extreme to recover our divine mission in life. Each day is an opportunity to raise ourselves to a higher level of awareness. By governing our thoughts, studying our motives, and communing with the Divine in meditation, we activate the divine spark placed in each soul by the Creator.

Prayer is truly important, and meditation is a sequel to prayer. As Bishop Sheen put it in his book *Lift Up Your Heart,* "Prayer is arduous when it is only a monologue, but it is a joy when our self-absorption gives way to the act of humbly listening."[5] By "the act of listening," the eminent cleric means meditation, for he clarifies, "For meditation, the ear of the soul is more important than the tongue: Saint Paul tells us that faith comes from listening." [6] In other words, meditation is like sending our soul-spark upward, seeking the Divine Light which radiates downward, enlightening us from within. Indeed, the Christ said, "You are the light of the world" (Matt. 5:14).

Meditation releases anxiety and emotional pain, and "the peace of God, which surpasses all understanding, will guard your hearts and minds through Christ Jesus" (Phil. 4:7). Meditation offers the opportunity to renew ourselves in spirit, which, in turn, brings peace and quiet determination. In the same way that nature renews itself with every sunrise, we also can daily renew ourselves by letting go of tensions and letting God reinvigorate our beings.

If we excuse our failures rather than seek to understand them, then we confine ourselves to a lower level of living—that of accepting our anger, laziness, and irritation as "the way we are." All of us have failed in some form or another. But have we studied the why? If not, discouragement waits at our door. Rather, why not persevere and try again, perhaps using a different angle? Also meditate to discover new energy and higher loves, and to release the tenacious insistence on *my way.* Result? We smile more, see the good in others, dare to be honest.

Meditation is one of the steps toward continuous self-improvement in all parts of life, with the aim of someday reaching perfection, as the Master ordered. Is there a limit to perfection? "In My Father's house are many mansions," said the Master, beckoning from the heavenward staircase leading to the soul's many mansions (John 14:2).

Most religions advocate loving God and loving our fellow man. People who actually practice these two principles find that they are happy, healthy, constructive individuals, for true happiness is an inside job and not based on outer material things.

On the other hand, those who run headlong after the selfish goals of fame, money, and power find themselves frustrated and ever anxious about the loss of selfish gain. Embezzlers and thieves live in fear of being found out. Such souls may have tenuously fattened their bank accounts, but these external-world trophies have lost for them the internal-world values that can't be seen. Consider the socially conscious teenager—the young lady who accepted a prom invitation from the football star, even though she'd previously accepted a date with another. She broke the first date—sneakily, so her family would not hear. She won her external-world trophy: recognition and fame as the date of the football star. Yet she'd lost the internal and eternal values of a virtuous character, and she incurred moral guilt. She also created for herself a conniving mind and deceitful heart. Such infractions of youth can become the blatant sins of later life. Such a person lives in dualism—selfishness striving against sincerity. This battle goes on in all of us. Studying our motives is the path toward self-understanding and peace of mind. External-world trophies pass away. Sterling character endures.

Eternal values can't be seen, yet only these bring lasting happiness. We can't see the invisible value of love, but we can see its manifestation as the mother cradles the child. We can't see the internal idea of self-centeredness, but we recognize it in the person demanding prompt service from a busy waiter. It's evident then that our actions come from the thought patterns inside of us, revealing scripture's wisdom. "For as he thinks in his heart, so is he" (Prov. 23:7). The father's loving thoughts bring gentle actions toward the toddler; the lustful person's thoughts produce fornication and adultery in our society. Good thoughts create harmony, and negative thoughts produce destruction. Why do we have wars and arguments? Let's study the world's mental condition. "Even so, every good tree bears good fruit, but a bad tree bears bad fruit. A good tree cannot bear bad fruit, nor can a bad tree bear good fruit. Every tree that does not bear good fruit is cut down and thrown into the fire. Therefore by their fruits you will know them" (Matt. 7:17–20). The fruits of mankind's anxious mental condition have contributed to our planet's stressful condition. However, the world can reverse its negative spiral downward by transforming its thought world. And the process begins within the mind and heart of each man, woman, and child. All souls can take part by reversing the negativism evident all around us. Three biblical concepts show us how each person can help elevate our world.

1. Meditate. Turn within, where higher or spiritual ideals can develop. These higher ideas can then govern the thoughts and actions of our days and nights. Listen for the Divine Heart, the inner Voice. "I will meditate on Your precepts, and contemplate Your ways" (Ps. 119:15).

2. Conduct a private daily inventory. Recognize each day where our steps have taken us. By studying our behavior, we can begin the process of changing failures to strengths. "Ponder the path of your feet, and let all your ways be established ... remove your foot from evil" (Prov. 4:26-27).

3. Be aware of our thoughts; train them. Direct our thoughts to higher planes and uplift others; do not tear them down. Rather, train ourselves to respond with wisdom, not with complaints and wisecracks. "I thought about my ways, and turned my feet to Your testimonies" (Ps. 119:59).

This, then, is the method of continuous self-improvement, with the ultimate aim of never-ending perfection:

1. Daily transformation of the mind and heart (meditation)
2. Daily study of how we behave and think (daily inventory)
3. Daily training of our thoughts to keep us on a positive path.

Self-improvement naturally results from this method of conscious awareness of our daily life. We do not become self-satisfied and dwell repeatedly on our successes; rather, we ask how the job could have been improved. In this way, we remain enthusiastic with ever-new goals, even in our senior years. Consider the businessman retiring and beginning his law degree, or the actor evolving into a movie producer, or a retired ballerina opening a dance academy. Grandma Moses, it is said, began painting at age seventy-five.[7] Some colleges offer senior discounts to those who simply want to learn more, not necessarily pursue a degree. There is always more to learn and deeper truths to discover.

As peeling an onion reveals new depth, so each thoughtful reading of scripture brings greater depth of perception. In the same way, we initially learn the grand sweep of the Bible before the mind grasps deeper insights. On the intellectual level, the third grader initially learns addition and subtraction, later learning multiplication and division. Eventually, his studies permit the understanding of algebra and geometry. On the spiritual level, our minds operate similarly. Our philosophical perceptions deepen through active love of neighbor, spiritual reading, prayer and meditation. As an example, after years of readings and reflections on the book of Genesis, this writer gained deeper perceptions. Initial readings gave the story's content: the *second* born was the favored son, not the first born. Abel, the second born of Adam and Eve and favored by God, was murdered by his jealous elder brother Cain. Also, Isaac, the second son of Abraham and Sarah, was favored by God above the first son, Ishmael, born of Sarah's slave woman and sent away from the family. And Jacob, the second-born twin, also received God's favor over the elder twin

Esau. God's hand rested on the second born in three succeeding generations. *Why is this so?* I wondered to myself. What spiritual insight can be found in these stories? What can we discern for our own spiritual growth?

One possibility is to realize that man generally focuses on his physical self before the spiritual self blossoms. Young children generally focus on their own personal and physical wishes. They require training to become considerate and unselfish. In the same way, the first born sons of Genesis mirror the selfishness and materialism of mankind's childhood stage. Cain was grasping, Ishmael was a "wild ass of a man," and Esau was a physically minded and carnally minded man. It was the second sons (Abel, Isaac, and Jacob) who grew in Godliness. In the same way, we must shed our grasping, self-centered, and materialistic selves before a spiritual nature can be set free to grow. Each of us can perceive individual deeper insights through spiritual reflection, for only the Almighty knows the next step in our personal climb upward toward Him. Creating a better world begins by creating one's own better self, the second-born (spiritual) self. This better self is the starting point for creating a better world. Because parts create the whole, the individual's part in restoring world harmony cannot be overemphasized.

We influence the world around us by our example in daily life. Are we examples of right living to our children or fellow employees or friends? Are we late for appointments and think nothing of it? Do we waste money by spending on impulse? Do we insist on our own way? Without fearlessly correcting our own selfishness, we cannot be salt for the earth. We teach best by example. As the Master exemplified what he taught, he advises us also "preach" by our personal example.: "Whosoever therefore breaks one of the least of these commandments, and teaches men so, shall be called least in the kingdom of heaven; but whoever does and teaches them, he shall be called great in the kingdom of heaven"(Matt. 5:19). Our slander and gossip teaches this behavior to children and pulls down the world. It takes personal *work* to stop this selfish behavior in ourselves and, instead, transform ourselves into worthy vessels of service. Have we honestly tried to become better people? When the Book of Life is opened, our greatest testimony will be our daily lives.

This writer has continued to endeavor to train herself over the years to think kindly toward others, regardless of their appearance. It's not easy to change habits of thinking. I used to have terribly unkind thoughts, using terms such as "old hag" for elderly women and "old fogy" for elderly men. I'm deeply ashamed to admit such unkindness. But I had to admit this to myself before I was able to overcome such arrogant, rude, and unkind thinking. Because of my preoccupation with eating, I judged overweight people, which actually reflected my own imbalanced state of mind. Then I learned about the significance of a person's thought life and became more aware of my mental criticism of others; the great shame hit hard. The next step was the mental battle of changing unkind thoughts to kind ones. Many ideas from my studies and reflections suddenly became meaningful. We are not to judge others, for we get back what we give, the readings had said. Then, instead of being judgmental, I began to wish for overweight people to find health and seek healthy lifestyles; and *I* needed to do the same thing! I sent compassionate thoughts to the sorrowful and goodwill to those around me. The result was finding myself more cheerful than ever before—and happier. Truly, thinking positively can create a more optimistic self, and thinking negatively, the opposite.

When the Master advocates our perfection, does he not mean our character perfection? Sterling character begins with the awareness of our personal set of values, what we consider acceptable in our thoughts and actions. The average person intellectually applauds the concepts of truth and honesty. Yet he likely thinks little about actually applying truth and honesty to his own behavior and to his own thinking. Do we excuse ourselves if we gossip, or lie, or cheat? Do we say, "I can't stand so-and-so," and justify it by saying, "Oh, everyone gossips"? Do we complain about the local and world situation, yet do nothing about it? We *can* do something about it simply by changing ourselves and setting the example of sterling character in thought and action. Instead of complaining about Sam or Mary, why not look for the good in them and speak kindly to them, help them feel a constructive purpose in their lives? Others would be influenced, for people admire goodness in others, and then imitate them.

Every area of our lives is an opportunity for self-study. How to begin?

1. We must turn within to the source of all energy and creativity. As Jesus said, "For indeed, the kingdom of God is within you" (Luke 17:21). How do we turn within? We sit comfortably, wear comfortable clothing, relax, close the eyes and ears, and turn the attention *inside* the mind. To quiet the racing thoughts circling in our heads, we might think of peaceful scenes of nature or images of the Divine. Then, like the rocket breaking through the hold of earthly gravity, our God-ward thoughts fly upward and break through the hold of worldly thoughts. We find peace, communing with the Divine.

2. We conduct a daily inventory of ourselves at the end of each day. Were we kind, or were our tempers short? Did selfish motives dominate, or were we patient, honest?

3. We train our thoughts to remain constructive and positive, rather than critical and condemning. Our minds are like broadcasting stations, radiating thoughts of encouragement and peace, or of the opposite—hatred, jealously, and greed. Let us tune in to God's wavelength and radiate its message of harmony.

Chapter 1
Meditation, or the Practice of Silence

Be still, and know that I am God
Psalms 46:10

Prayer is a familiar term to most people, although not everyone prays. The Lord's Prayer (Matt. 6:9) is likely the most well-known prayer in the English language.

Meditation is a more advanced stage of prayer and proceeds *from* prayer. In prayer, we *talk to* God; in meditation, we *listen to* him. The Bible tells us Jesus prayed, and doubtless he also meditated, for in the Gospels, many times we read about such instances. For example:

"When He had sent the multitudes away, He went up on a mountain by Himself to pray" (Matt. 14:23);

"When He had sent them away, He departed to the mountain to pray" (Mark 6:46);

"And it happened, as He was alone praying, that His disciples joined Him" (Luke 9:18);

"He departed again to a mountain by Himself alone" (John 6:15).

Prayer turns into meditation when we turn our whole mind and heart *within*, where God is, and *listen*. Indeed, the Savior told us, "The kingdom of God does not come with observation; nor will they say, 'See here!' or 'See there!' For indeed, the kingdom of God is within you" (Luke 17:20–21).

Meditation is sometimes called mental prayer or mental relaxation. It consists of turning our conscious minds from the outer world of matter (or macrocosm) to the interior world of mind (microcosm). Simply put, we place our whole attention on the spiritual dimension

1

of ourselves, and resting in God, we listen. As the Master said, "He who has ears to hear, let him hear" (Luke 8:8).

Listening or resting in God, however, is not easy because the mind naturally swings outward to the material world. To pull the attention inward to the spirit is a difficult job and means disciplining the senses. Thoughts of money problems, for example, might bombard the meditator or fretfulness about a work project or about someone's comment. If *these* thoughts can be dismissed, then other thoughts attack, such as anxiety about the room's temperature or an itchy spot on the ankle. Focusing attention wholly on the Divine is not easy. Some souls readily fly to meditation and encounter minimal trouble. This writer is the opposite—after forty years, I still struggle. Yet a more serene spirit always follows meditation. The effort itself brings a reward.

The Divine Master told us how to begin prayer (personal, interior prayer): "But you, when you pray, go into your room, and when you have shut your door, pray to your Father who is in the secret place" (Matt. 6:6). We can do this physically by finding a quiet room and closing the door.

And we can also do this nearly anywhere by finding the quiet room within ourselves; we pull our *attention* inward and shut the door of our physical senses—the eyes from sight, the ears from sound, and the physical senses from taste, touch, and smell.

This method of improving our concentration draws us closer to the Kingdom of God within. We turn away thoughts of dinner, money, or anxiety of any kind. We concentrate instead on Divine Love coming from the eternal heart of God. The result? We find ourselves refreshed and rejuvenated, with an awareness of our oneness with creation and its creatures. We emerge as souls better able to serve God through serving others. We laugh with them more generously, greet them more genuinely.

And meditation brings bonus values as well.

- Our concentration improves in other areas of life, for meditation helps us to sustain thoughts in one direction. The student studies more readily, the musician plays more easily, concentration in any area flows more naturally.

Science verifies that higher, positive brain waves operate for those who meditate. "The long-term practice of love-focused meditation can change the baseline state of our brains. Or simply put, thinking positive thoughts can make us feel happier," states *Positive Thinking* magazine.[8] In the article titled "The Joy of Meditation," the brain activity of Buddhist Monks seeking unconditional loving kindness toward all beings was compared to that of students' brain activity as they meditated. Using magnetic resonance imaging, results showed that students' brain activity during meditation increased slightly, while the monks' brain activity during meditation was extremely high in the left prefrontal lobe, which lights up when we are happy. After meditation, this brain area remained more active in the monks than in the students. That is, increased positive thinking produced a happier state of mind.

- Our health improves as we experience increased peace and release of tension. Indeed, men of science now acknowledge that constructive, positive thinking also influences bodily health. Since thoughts themselves cannot be scientifically measured, physicians and scientists can only measure the *results* of those who live with optimistic (not pessimistic) feelings and attitudes. Physicians have published books to recount this astonishing phenomenon. For example, Dr. Mehmet Oz stated, "I cannot overstate the importance of a patient's attitude toward his or her illness and the long road to recovery ... the mind must help the body."[9] And Dr. Bernie Siegel adds that "the power of suggestion, while not a panacea, was a worthy ally of pharmacy, surgery, and hygiene,"[10] and that "patients whose rooms faced an open courtyard, a tree, and the sky got well faster than those whose rooms faced a brick wall."[11] Dr. Siegel speaks of Dr. William S. Sadler, who was convinced that the mind has equal partnership with drug-based cures. Moreover Dr. John Schindler has noted that "good emotions are your best medicine," basing his opinion on the scientific study of emotions related to health.[12]

- Our intuition improves through meditation. We feel ourselves guided into right paths. Many people today attest to this inner awareness. We sense something telling us not to purchase this "bargain." Conversely, we feel compelled to pursue the harder path, despite others' scorn. Where do these insights come from? From the Unseen World of Higher Souls, whose guidance becomes interiorly audible to the meditator's listening ear.

- We become less fearful. Why is this so? Because in the act of meditation, we turn away from worldly anxieties. And when we let go of anxieties, God can draw them *out* of us. It's a law of physics. Hold on to something, and the hold is there. Release the hold, and the release takes place. But after the release, the void must be filled with something else. In meditation, tensions are replaced by peace, anxieties by euphoria. We become more compassionate, kindly souls.

Why is meditation not practiced more? Because we generally focus only on our physical and emotional selves. However, the spiritual ingredient needs to be consciously developed. Christ told us, "God is Spirit, and those who worship Him must worship in spirit and in truth" (John 4:24). Therefore, we need to create a place for spirituality in our daily lives.

Perhaps one of the hardest parts of meditation is establishing the time for it. I had to literally schedule meditation into the day as a priority in order to "make it happen." Since I lived alone, this was a private matter for me; no one had to know. During this period, the phone or doorbell went unheeded. The morning rising hour and evening bedtime were carefully planned to ensure a meditation period before beginning the day's activities and before retiring at night. Sometimes other activities had to have a limit, such as when to turn off the television, close the book, or leave a social gathering. Truly, if a person believes in the value of meditation, doing it is not a burden. As the Master said, "Take My yoke upon you and learn from Me … for My yoke is easy and My burden is light" (Matt. 11:29–30).

While economic needs are indeed a dominant factor in most lives, people today rarely place a daily priority on a private spiritual time. Until we do, an interior void exists which cannot be filled with exterior things. And when these exterior things fail to satisfy, we seek a greater variety or more intensity of them. We buy the newest type of phone, find another partner, seek another drink. Yet dissatisfaction continues and grows. Losing ourselves in the exterior world never brings satisfaction, never fills the spiritual void.

Devoting time to the spiritual is a directive thousands of years old. The Ten Commandments given to Moses include "Remember the Sabbath day, to keep it holy" (Exod. 20:8). Also, Genesis tells us God rested on the seventh day. The Creator modeled for us a balance of the physical and spiritual elements as part of healthy living. In our busy days, we can release tension and find daily spiritual rejuvenation by meditation. But disciplining ourselves to schedule time for it each day requires commitment. Sadly, much of mankind concentrates entirely on the material world and forgets its Maker. Those who ignore a spiritual dimension generally move faster and faster on the worldly plane—and then can't understand why they suffered a nervous breakdown.

We have time for what is important to us. Moses acknowledged this by ensuring the ancient Hebrews gave time and attention to their spiritual heritage. They wore phylacteries (bands or coils on the arms) to remind them of prayer. The daily life of the Israelites included constant physical reminders of the One who led them out of Egyptian slavery. God established the designation of "clean" and "unclean" food (Lev. 11) as well as personal cleanliness habits (Lev. 15). Numerous rules of conduct were established (Lev. 19), and continual rituals and holy festivals were observed (Num. 28–29), especially the annual Day of Atonement (Lev. 16). In addition, the ancient Israelites were to put tassels on the corners of their garments to remind them to keep the Lord's commandments (Num. 15:37–40).

Today we schedule dentist appointments, doctor appointments, and auto repair appointments. But do we schedule our daily spiritual appointments, such as time for spiritual reading and meditation?

Our appointment with God in meditation should be a pleasant experience. We might pinpoint our style of preference in the meditation steps offered below.

Steps in Meditation

1. People prepare to meditate in various ways, and we should use the option that appeals to our nature. Meditation in a group has the powerful benefit of joined hearts and minds seeking God, for indeed Jesus the Christ said, "Where two or three are gathered together in My name, I am there in the midst of them" (Matt. 18:20). Yet practicality deems individual meditation appropriate in many cases. Still, every meditation is powerful. To prepare for meditation, it's good to refocus ourselves from the cares of the outward daily life to the inward self, the realm of the soul. We may repeat a prayer or read, perhaps.

• Psalms 23, 91, and 138 are favorites.

• Read the words of Jesus, such as Chapter 14 in the Gospel of John or The Sermon on the Mount (Matt. 5–7).

• Read a miracle of Jesus and visualize every detail—the weather, colors, sounds, expressions on faces.

• Pray from your heart the Lord's Prayer or a prayer of your own.

2. Establish a place of quiet. Some people prefer, instead of total silence, to hear peaceful music that soothes the soul. Others seek the silence within in order to hear the voice of the Divine Heart. Individual preferences vary.

3. Use a comfortable chair. Some people prefer an upright chair, while others select a recliner. However, it's best not to lie down, as this position induces sleep.

4. Sit in a relaxed position to facilitate complete concentration.

5. Consciously relax individual sections of the body without haste. Some people can feel the relaxation better by saying, without haste, "I *relax* my feet (pause); I *relax* my legs (pause); I *relax* my abdomen (pause); I *relax* my chest (pause); I *relax* my arms (pause); I *relax* my neck (pause); I *relax* my head (pause); my body is completely relaxed."

6. Sit quietly and focus on your breathing. Breathe gently— in and out. During inhalation some people mentally say words, such as "Peace" or "Truth." Then during exhalation, they say, "*Release* anxiety" or "*Release* tension."

7. How long should you meditate? If you are not used to meditating, begin with a daily ten-minute session the first week, and move to fifteen minutes the second week. Eventually, allow yourself a thirty-minute period. Deep peacefulness is often the result. But results come gradually. Meditation is a process, like the growth of a child. Daily changes may not be apparent, but the divine energy is stirring within the soul, nonetheless.

8. The purpose of the meditation period is to deepen *personal* communion with the living God. The saints of old devoted one-on-one time to God and produced results. Moses was on Mount Sinai for forty days and descended with the tablets bearing the Ten Commandments. His face was radiant as a result of being in the Presence of The Lord (Exod. 34:28–35). Isaiah journeyed to the Holy Mountain where God spoke in a whisper within his soul, not in the

earthquake or the wind; he descended with renewed vigor to combat pagan worshippers (1 Kings 19:1–18). Alone on the Isle of Patmos, Saint John received the words of the Book Revelation while "in spirit," or in meditation (Rev. 1:10–11). In the thirteenth-century liberation of France, Saint Joan of Arc continually prayed in churches by herself as she led the Dauphin's royal army to victory against the English soldiers.[13] These saints experienced personal communion with God and changed the world.

9. People use different methods to help them concentrate or focus their minds. Some people visualize the Divine Beloved surrounded by a radiant light. Others picture a golden beam extending from the crown of the head upward to the heavens. Some people mentally repeat peaceful words, such as "Jesus," or "*Thy* will be done, not mine," or other brief words helpful to each particular person.

If the mind tends to jump around like a monkey, let us persevere, for results will come. Our minds are different, and meditation is easier for some than for others. If the mind wanders, gently pull it back without self-condemnation. By gently returning to our chosen spiritual focus, we will develop deeper concentration. In the Divine Presence, peacefulness descends and we emerge from meditation as souls renewed, for we've been spiritually nourished by the Bread of Heaven.

10. When should we meditate? Morning meditation is especially helpful (before or after breakfast), for meditation focuses our mind on higher aims. Then, throughout the day we find ourselves more relaxed, less anxious.

Meditation before bed is also beneficial. With thoughts turned Above, we are bound to slumber more peacefully and arise refreshed, ready for a new day.

Daily practice of meditation is important. As a growing garden needs daily water, our spiritual life needs daily Living Waters from the Divine in meditation. Eventually, we find ourselves happier, healthier people with a higher focus directing our life.

The practice of daily meditation enables our spiritual selves to blossom. We see the good in others, rather than sending wordless darts of criticism, which may be the habit of many people. Instead, we become more loving—effortlessly. Show love to others and it comes back. Criticize, and it comes back to us as well. This universal truth was affirmed by Saint Paul, who said, "For whatever a man sows, that he will also reap" (Gal. 6:7).

Giving time each day to meditation balances our physical selves with our spiritual selves, and greater harmony comes to our bodies, minds, and souls.

Chapter 2
Daily Inventory

I thought about my ways,
and turned my feet to Your testimonies.
Psalms 119:59

Today's world promotes talking as a means of solving problems, and this method has merit. Verbalizing our anxiety allows a catharsis or purging of our pain. This form of release has proven its value individually and in groups. Individually, some souls seek peace and spiritual help in church confessionals. And others spend precious dollars seeking advice from professional counselors, while friends talk to friends as a regular way to express concern and vent anxieties. Also, group discussions help us solve problems as well, such as support groups where people tell their stories and find relief. The boss holds staff meetings; school principles gather teachers; married couples go to counselors. Indeed, these are all valid actions.

There remains another inner method, as yet untapped by many. Because each of us is the Chief Executive Officer (CEO) of our own inner organization, why not call a staff meeting for the managers of our own internal physical, emotional, and mental selves? Just as a shopkeeper takes a daily inventory to ensure the solvency of his business, we can take a daily inventory of our mind-body-soul corporations to see if we are morally sound or accruing debt toward others, near or far. The prudent person listens to his bodily stress and anguished conscience, which whispers transgressions of the moral law. As CEO of ourselves, we would do well to realize that every internal operational failure (physical or mental) comes from an earlier cause. The law of cause and effect operates on all levels of creation.

This universal law of cause and effect is sometimes called God's law of reward and punishment. But "punishment" may unwittingly come from our own hands because of our deviation from the Law, bringing on negative consequences. "What law?" some might ask. The commandments presented in the Bible are the natural laws of a harmonious universe. Any deviation from this harmony produces discord. The principle of cause and effect is the same in all times and places. Thus we have the Eastern term "karma," which is the same idea as the psalmist's words: "You render to each one according to his work" (Ps. 62:12). What we do comes back to us. Be deceitful to others, and somewhere along the way we will be the victims of deceit. Why? Our failure to act righteously causes us to have to learn the "hard way"—by experience. That is, we must suffer unkindness at the hands of others in order to empathize with the suffering *of* others. If we refuse to act honestly toward others, the universal hand of God has to teach us the lesson of honesty by bitter experience. Some children only learn by pain, and sometimes we are the same way. This is when bitter experience can redirect us to the path of harmonious living.

I learned my wrong-eating lesson by bitter pain. First there was the social pain of needing psychiatric care, and then came the daily emotional pain of struggling to keep the "eating monster" in check. I followed professional guidance to curb my imbalanced habits, such as eating slowly and chewing fully. These practices helped me look beyond the enjoyment of taste to something greater—namely, the enjoyment of freedom from slavery to food. But such realizations do not occur overnight. They are the result of self-honesty and self-discipline. I am convinced that the daily practices of meditation, self-inventory, and thought training have saved my life. These practices gave me a three-step daily package for self-awareness and self-control. My deep-seated problems and entrenched poor habits caused me to have to learn by pain.

Biblical characters also learned via pain. In Genesis, Jacob tricked his father and cheated his brother out of his lawful inheritance—their father's inheritance and blessing. Later, Jacob himself fell victim to a deceitful father-in-law's trickery and worked an extra seven years to acquire his chosen bride. "What goes around comes around" is a truth deeper than we might imagine.

The universal law of cause and effect operates in the unseen realm. As an example, the unjust action of Person A toward Person B is seen by the Cosmic Recording Angel, or by the karmic law that always operates. Somewhere along the way, Person A himself will experience injustice; he has caused himself to have to learn by bitter experience, since he would not accept the words of Universal Teachings and Teachers. The painful lesson may not come immediately, but it will come nonetheless. The ancient Israelites who failed to honor God's commandments experienced moral decline and loss of unity. As a result, they were conquered and deported from Israel and Judah. In their suffering, they turned again to God, the giver of universal truths presented in the moral laws of the Five Books of Moses. The Jews repented and were restored to their homeland, but subsequently turned away again from God and again suffered bitterly. Each of us repeats this cycle until, by painful lessons, we remain strong in adhering to Universal Law, or other moral teachings such as the Ten Commandments. Jesus encapsulated the Ten Commandments in his two Great Commandments: "'You shall love the Lord your God with all your heart, with all your soul, and with all your mind.' This is the first and great commandment. And the second is like it: 'You shall love your neighbor as yourself.' On these two commandments hang all the Law and the Prophets" (Matt. 22:37–40).

A personal daily inventory identifies our failures to honor God and neighbor. Patterns of daily tensions emerge and show us where to seek self-understanding. Perhaps a daily inventory can be better understood by focusing on it through the Five Ws: what, why, when, where, and who.

1. What is a daily inventory?
   It is a review of our day in terms of our emotional state and our moral/ethical conduct.

2. Why do it?
Self-growth is the way to keep enthusiastic and interested in life. While some people may be content as they are, others may feel trapped by their jobs or environments. All circumstances present an opportunity for self-revelation and reflection, asking ourselves our part in the happy or unhappy state of affairs. But self-study takes bravery and perseverance, for facing ourselves is not easy. We unmask our true desires and identify deeper motives. With humility, we then *redirect* our thoughts and actions into uplifting channels. The wisdom of Proverbs 3:13 tells us, "Happy is the man who finds wisdom, and the man who gains understanding." Similarly, happy is the man who creates a sterling character and gains self-understanding by a daily self-inventory.

3. When do we conduct this self-assessment?
The best time is the end of the day, though we can jot notes at any time.

4. Where do we write our thoughts?
Many people have an established place, using a notebook with dated entries, but the location can be any spot where distractions will not interfere with sincere thought.

5. Who does the writing?
The writing is completely personal and private, for only we know our true motives and desires. We keep our own casebooks, and no one else needs to read them.

How do we proceed? Daily inventories come in many styles, and we should select the one that appeals to us, or create our own. Some methods are outlined below:

1. **Daily Inventory Using The Five Basic Needs**
According to a college psychology professor (my guide and mentor), the ancient physician and philosopher Patanjali stated

that man has five basic needs: physical, vital, psychological, intellectual, and philosophical or spiritual. Current sociologists may agree with these concepts, though their choice of label may vary.

These five basic needs apply to every soul in all locations and centuries. Balancing these needs in a universal manner brings growth and happiness. These needs can help us aim at consciously chosen goals. Otherwise, we may react to momentary whims or by emotion—rather than a balance of reason *and* emotion.

a.   Physical Need

Physical needs are those things a person needs to achieve his/her goals. We require shelter from the elements and tools for our work. The caveman used animal skins; today we use clothes. Transportation, appliances, furniture, and technological devices are important today. But we must determine the difference between needs and wants. Is a second car truly a need or simply a convenience? Is having the newest model essential? Is the new dress a need or merely on sale? Wise, unselfish use of assets given by the Divine requires honest thought, for achieving our goals might mean limiting expenditures. Following a champagne appetite with only a beer income spells difficulty, if not disaster. The indiscriminate use of credit cards may be taken as an example in today's world. Youthful college students who have not been responsibly trained may find themselves disastrously in debt. It would help us all to seek the loftier goal of good character rather than the indiscriminate purchase of any worldly item.

Daily Inventory:
Are the things I wish to have genuine needs or merely "wants"?
Am I being greedy or stingy?

b.   Vital Needs
These are elements the body needs to stay alive: air, water, food, exercise, sleep, sunshine. We generally take these for granted, thinking little about them. Proper nutrition and adequate exercise

can promote health. Yet many people ignore these facts daily and follow old habit patterns, witnessed by the high rate of obesity, even in children. Most of us could be healthier if we worked at it. How many people could include an exercise program in their lives but don't? How many people stay up too late watching videos or sitting at the computer? How many of us routinely consume the sugary or fatty foods swamping store counters today? Real effort is required to take charge of our lives by creating healthy eating habits and following a disciplined schedule of proper exercise and sleep. Are we willing to face this and do something about it? I know an excessively overweight young woman with two small children. She seemed unable to control her eating habits, routinely devouring highly caloric foods at inappropriate occasions. Yet happily, today she seems to be taking control of her life, and her size has begun to significantly normalize.

Daily Inventory:
Am I doing essential things to improve my health? If not, why not?
Is it "too hard" to change eating habits, sleeping habits? Why?
Am I exercising enough? If not, why not?

c.   Psychological Need

This need involves having proper companionship and love in our lives. We benefit by associating with those who make us feel comfortable. Even on a school playground, children of like natures naturally gravitate to each other. Something attracts us, or not, to those around us. We feel secure in *belonging* somewhere and knowing someone cares. Witness the child who yearns to excel at something in order to receive parental praise. Even a wife responds to appreciative words for the good dinner she prepared. In Charles Dickens's tale *A Christmas Carol*, Bob Cratchit proclaimed the dessert "a wonderful pudding!" as it blazed "in half-a-quartern of ignited brandy." His wife had her doubts, but then sighed a relief.[14] But we may not be surrounded by loved ones at certain times of our lives. When a sense of loneliness or unhappiness occurs we should be spurred to ask why, and the thinking person begins a self-analysis (daily inventory).

When answers are hard to find, meditation brings new ideas and a release of stress.

Daily Inventory:
Do I have good friends? Am I a good friend to others?
Do I have love in my life? Do I show love to others?

d.   Intellectual need

Intellectual need is a person's self-expression and has nothing to do with a high school diploma or college degree. Doing what brings joy and satisfaction is different for each of us. A daily inventory can reveal when we are most happy. The pianist needs to be associated with music, the physician with healing techniques, the carpenter with physical structures. Yet, the activity that brings us joy could bring insufficient income. So, the aspiring writer might need to earn a living as a store cashier while writing at night, but the aim of publication is never lost. The would-be actor who performs at the local playhouse discovers a satisfaction not present in his daily job. Finding a constructive outlet for an innate desire or talent brings a burst of joy and zeal. Life is no longer boring. The woman who darns socks or knits while watching TV is being productive and creative. TV is not a time-waster.

Our self-expression should benefit mankind and bring personal fulfillment. Unfortunately, the world situation often reflects a selfish use of intellect to increase one's pocketbook or power. Yet greed can never fully satisfy the human heart. The conscience stubbornly persists, and even atheists and murderers have been known to call for a priest at life's end.

The daily inventory helps us discover the self-expression that will bring true fulfillment and uplift the world.

Daily Inventory
Am I doing what I would like to do? If not, why not?
Am I continuing to grow by learning new things?

e.   Philosophical or Spiritual Need

Excavations of civilizations since ancient times have revealed man's inborn quest for union with an unknown power that runs the universe. Even our microscopes, test tubes, and space explorations cannot reveal the spark of life, the ruling force that keeps the planets in orbit and our bodies intact. Harmony is on God's side; the worldly destructive forces are the work of man. Each person needs an explanation of his relationship to others and this Ruling Power. Universal religions have helped many find inner peace, no matter the turmoil of life around them. Harold Begbie's *Broken Earthenware* tells the true story of a recovering alcoholic who had found hope with members of the Salvation Army. Yet one night he arrived home drunk again. The "Puncher," as he was called, fled to his Salvation Army jersey and donned it; under the flag of its protection, he felt safe. Though difficulties deepened for him, he never fell to drink again.[15] This writer too has found solace and inner strength simply by sitting in a church sanctuary, a sure haven of peace in the stressfulness of life.

Daily Inventory
Which motive guides me daily? The Golden Rule or the "me-first"
rule?
Do I lie or cheat? Do I justify it?
Do I tell the truth and keep my word? If not, why not?

Each person has to find his own relationship with the Divine. We can help each other along the way, and should. But in the end, each soul has to personally respond to God's call, or choose not to respond. Daily meditation and daily inventory provide a path for the true seeker of a higher, happier, more harmonious level of living. The daily inventory reminds us to keep universal values first, not money. Money is a tool for accomplishing constructive goals for the good of all.

2. **Daily Inventory Using Development of Desirable Characteristics**
   In this method of daily inventory we do four things:

   * create a list of traits that would help us improve our character

- establish new habits to develop the trait in our lives

- make a chart to track our daily efforts

- mark the chart and study our progress

For example, we could develop a chart such as the following:

Trait to Develop	How to Do This	Did this? (Y or N)
Eat right amount	Decide the amount before the meal	
Chew fully		
Use good manners		
Do not eat between meals		
Exercise	Three times a week: walk or bike, etc.	
Sleep enough	Establish a bedtime, stick to it	
Be calm before bed		
Be kind	Open doors for others	
Greet people cheerfully		
Don't gossip		
Don't interrupt		
Be on time		
Look for ways to be considerate		
Be honest	Apologize when wrong	
Don't cheat		
Don't steal		

The pursuit of moral perfection is nothing new. Benjamin Franklin's famous *Autobiography* details a similar method .[16] Thus we are not alone in creating our own list and recording our progress.

Benjamin Franklin's List of 13 Virtues

1.   TEMPERANCE

Eat not to dullness; drink not to elevation.

2.   SILENCE

Speak not but what may benefit others or yourself; avoid trifling conversation.

3.   ORDER

Let all your things have their places; let each part of your business have its time.

4.   RESOLUTION

Resolve to perform what you ought; perform without fail what you resolve.

5.   FRUGALITY

Make no expense but to do good to others or yourself; i.e., waste nothing.

6.   INDUSTRY

Lose no time; be always employed in something useful; cut off all unnecessary actions.

7.   SINCERITY

Use no hurtful deceit; think innocently and justly, if you speak, speak accordingly.

8.   JUSTICE

Wrong none by doing injuries, or omitting the benefits that are your duty.

9.   MODERATION

Avoid extremes; forbear resenting injuries so much as you think they deserve.

10.   CLEANLILNESS

Tolerate no uncleanliness in body, clothes, or habitation.

11.   TRANQUILITY

Be not disturbed at trifles, or at accidents common or unavoidable.

12.   CHASTITY

Rarely use venery but for health or offspring, never to dullness, weakness, or the injury of your own or another peace or reputation.

13.   HUMILITY

Imitate Jesus and Socrates.

Above is Benjamin Franklin's list of 13 virtues for character improvement. Mr. Franklin added his personal definition of each virtue. During a period of his life, Mr. Franklin paid daily attention to developing these virtues in his character and recorded his progress in a small notebook.

Example of Benjamin Franklin's Page of One of the Virtues

TEMPERANCE

EAT NOT TO DULLNESS;

DRINK NOT TO ELEVATION.

/	SUN	MON	TUE	WED	THU	FRI	SAT/
TEMPERANCE							
SILENCE	*	*	/	*		/	/
ORDER	**	*	*		*	*	*
RESOLUTION/			*		*	/	
FRUGALITY		*			*		
INDUSTRY			*				
SINCERITY							
JUSTICE							
MODERATION							
CLEANLINESS							
TRANQUILITY							
CHASTITY							
HUMILITY							

Above is a partially completed page of Benjamin Franklin's notebook. He allotted a page for one virtue for a week, shown by the headings at the top of the chart. He concentrated on strengthening that virtue during the week and allowed failures in other virtues to occur as they may. Above, his notebook shows that "temperance" is clear of errors (black marks) but infractions of other virtues occurred. Every 13 weeks, he would be able to complete a full course of a week's attention to each of the 13 virtues. In this method, he could complete 4 courses a year and he hoped one day his notebook would be entirely free of black marks. Although he never succeeded, Mr. Franklin records that he was a better person for having tried.

What a marvelous tool! Imagine what a better world it would be if each person really *tried* daily to develop sterling character to rid himself of unkindness, dishonesty, and greed. We may not reach perfection in this life, but we are better souls for having made the

21

effort. And after all, life is eternal; thus we can keep improving, keep climbing to a higher mansion prepared for us, as Jesus promised in John's Gospel, Chapter 14.

3. **Daily Inventory Using the Seven Cardinal Sins and the Seven Cardinal Virtues**
    These famous lists provide another tool for daily self-examination. The method is twofold:

    *   Eliminate one of the Cardinal Sins in our lives

    *   Replace it with one of the Cardinal Virtues. For example, undue pride would be replaced with humility.

Two classic lists are below, although variations exist. Pope Gregory the Great originated the following enumeration of The Seven Cardinal Sins in the sixth century, and it was accepted by Thomas Aquinas and many other theologians.[17] The list below of The Seven Cardinal Virtues reflects variations found on Web sites and is the version derived from my mentor. I have chosen to use his list of virtues, since it has helped me for over thirty years in my daily self-analyses.

Seven Cardinal Sins	Seven Cardinal Virtues
Pride	Faith
Avarice (greed)	Fortitude
Lust	Patience
Envy	Perseverance
Gluttony	Humility
Anger	Justice
Sloth (laziness)	Temperance
	(Also, Charity and Spirituality/ Chastity)

Having a list of "sins" designated for us might help us recognize areas where we need improvement. Similarly, a list of "virtues" can guide us to higher paths of character development. For example, we can replace anger with patience, or gluttony with temperance (moderation in eating or drinking).

One key to success in all methods is discovering *why* we failed in some area. The next step is doing something to prevent further failure. For instance, by reflecting on the Cardinal Sin of undue pride in our lives, we might discover our habit of gossiping or mentally criticizing others. Then we think about *why* we do this. Does the person cause us to be angry? Why? Are we secretly jealous? If so, why? What good does the criticism do? Are we helping anyone by this? Or, do we want the spotlight for a moment? Do we feel bad about engaging in gossip? If not, why not? For we have been warned, "Judge not, that you be not judged. For with what judgment you judge, you will be judged; and with the measure you use, it will be measured back to you. And why do you look at the speck in your brother's eye, but do not consider the plank in your own eye?" (Matt. 7:1–3).

Why not become alert when arrogant feelings come or unkind criticism pops out by habit? That is the first step in self-awareness. The sin of pride occurs frequently in our society. However, we can help make the world better by making ourselves better. How? By sincerely practicing the Golden Rule. Do we want others to selfishly criticize us? If not, we should stop criticizing others. Instead of harping on their faults, we should send them wishes of healing and goodness. Peace and love throughout the whole world begin with peace and love in each individual heart. The superior person builds others up; the lesser person tears them down.

Let's look more deeply at each of the Seven Cardinal Sins:

Pride, in its negative form, is destructive. This is not the rightful pride one feels for the child who earned an A in school or who served honorably in military conflict. Rather, it is the undue pride in ourselves, for it is destructive and manifests itself in various forms of conceit. Recall the arrogant Pharisee who prayed, "God, I thank You that I am not like other men are—extortionists, unjust, adulterers, or even this tax collector. I fast twice a week, and I give tithes of all that I possess" (Luke 18:11–12). Jesus contrasted the scornful pride of this Pharisee with the humble prayer of the sinner who dared not raise his eyes above as he prayed, "God be merciful to me a sinner" (Luke 18:11–13). Do we catch ourselves looking with contempt on others' clothing or manners? If so, we mirror the arrogant Pharisee. All of us come from different backgrounds and we likely differ in our opinions. Prideful judgment of another is the antithesis of being objective, compassionate, and respectful. These latter traits are desirable for the aspirant of universal living.

Pride can also manifest itself in the desire for recognition. This sin shouts wordlessly to the world, "Look at me and what I have done!" It is the immature mind that wants attention. The soul who focuses on "what others think" cannot simultaneously focus on following the universal virtue of righteousness. Any honor or success we experience comes from God, as Solomon reminds us: "The blessing of the Lord makes one rich, and He adds no sorrow with it" (Prov. 10:22). Have we worked hard and honestly to achieve success? If so, it was the Universal Hand of God that brought our efforts to fruition and gave us this experience in order for us to evolve. But success should not be twisted and bring conceit. James shows us the proper attitude: "Humble yourselves in the sight of the Lord, and He will lift you up" (James 4:10).

What we are and what we have come from the Power Above and can be changed at any time. Witness homes lost in floods or wildfires. Witness jobs lost or life savings dissolved. We experience suffering for reasons beyond our knowledge, for we do not know God's wider plan. Nonetheless, we can share Job's trust: "The Lord gave, and the Lord has taken away; blessed be the name of the Lord" (Job 1:21). Like Job, we may have lost everything yet still remain true to God, vowing, "Though He slay me, yet I will trust in Him" (Job 13:15). Saint Paul's beautiful treatise provides solace in the midst of sorrows: "All things work together for good to those who love God, to those who are the called according to His purpose" (Rom. 8:28). My own failure to be promoted to lieutenant colonel in the U.S. Army seemed the end of the world at the time. And even my first effort at finding a job after Army retirement failed. Eventually I moved to New Mexico, where greater spiritual advancement has occurred in my life than in the previous thirty years. Thus, what seems "bad" may turn out well in the long run.

Avarice shows itself in greed for things we want but do not need, or in excessive accumulation of money or assets. Do we "have to have" the extra coat or newest gadget? Practicing contentment is one of the greatest ways to find peace. Our external desires are never completely satisfied, for there is always a new model or better product.

Avarice also reveals itself in stinginess with money and reflects attachment to material goods; fear of losing them becomes a source of insecurity. Why do we cling to material goods? Are we fearful of "not having"? There must be a reason for this. We should recall the widow who used her last bit of food to feed the prophet Elijah who, in turn, rewarded her with a bin of flour and jar of oil that never ran dry during her period of need (1 Kings 17:10–16).

Divine Providence provides help for the righteous and ferrets out wrongdoers, though we may not personally witness the workings of Ultimate Justice—for it truly exists, as steadfast as the daily rising sun. It is well to remember the wisdom of scripture: "He who walks with integrity walks securely, but he who perverts his ways will become known" (Prov. 10:9). Avarice can take the form of pocketing money from the cash register at work or, on a grander scale, misappropriating funds for personal use or abuse. Scandals like this, in government or corporations, have been in the news. That is, we take more than what is proper. This form of avarice shows attachment to the material world or to our "place" in society. Not having the needed money, we steal to acquire it and justify our "need" under loftier titles of "good business" or getting "our share."

Yet there are those who do right because doing so is *right*, who do a good job for the good job's sake. To such people the unseen values of Goodness have greater attraction than the worldly glitter of name and fame that fades away. The Master from Nazareth could look beyond the exterior of a person into his heart, which mirrored the true merit of a man.

Lust is an imbalanced desire for pleasures of the flesh. It can manifest as addiction to pornography or indulgence in unlawful sex—an act which has led to discord since the beginning of history. Sexual fulfillment is a God-given pleasure and results in harmony when it is lawfully expressed within the bonds of heterosexual marriage. But the undisciplined soul can readily succumb to the snare of sexual attraction. With immorality on the rise, the world today merely blinks an eye at this sin and accepts it as a normal part of "civilized" society. In more honest moments, though, the carnally minded soul quietly respects the virtuous person, for the moral laws are written on all our hearts. Yet many proclaim their right to do whatever they want because they are, as yet, unwilling to restrain their promiscuous habits. Even King David fell to this sin. Seeing another man's wife bathing on a balcony, David experienced the fatal attraction and succumbed to his lust for Bathsheba. Using a king's power, he called for this beautiful woman to be brought to the palace, then ordered Bathsheba's husband to the front lines of battle where he would be killed. David could then "legally" add a new wife to his family. Yet later, the words of Nathan the prophet tinged David's conscience and drew forth his confession. And David's psalms of remorse are recorded for all to see (specifically, Psalms 6, 32, 38, 51, 102, 130, and 143.) Bishop Sheen writes that "David's remorse then became the occasion of his rebirth to both individual justice and social justice; he composed the Seven Penitential Psalms, crying out, in the agony of a soul that was beginning to find its peace: 'Have mercy on me, O Lord; have mercy on me.'" [18] Jesus commented on just this problem for mankind: "If your eye causes you to sin, pluck it out and cast it from you" (Matt. 5:29). The Master never meant a literal interpretation, naturally, but He recognized that lust begins in the mind. To prevent impure thinking, we need to keep our eyes pure, for untamed thought can lead to untamed action.

Envy cannot endure to see the goodness or success of others. The envious person camouflages his jealousy many times by tearing down the achievements of others. Have we felt jealous or envious of another? If so, there is a choice to make. We can be critical, or we can salute the other's success and be inspired to pursue the path meant for us. The latter choice requires hard work. Thus the jealous soul, unwilling to face his deficiencies and unwilling to change, would rather criticize others than create a better character for himself. Because King Saul envied the popularity of young David, he sought to hunt down and kill his rival. This jealousy led to the king's downfall, for the universal law of cause and effect will not let wrong action go unpunished. King Saul could have overcome his jealousy, but he didn't (1 Sam. 18–31). William Shakespeare, an excellent portrayer of human emotions, ably shows how envy can destroy relationships and life itself. The tragedy of *Othello* depicts envious Iago seeking the destruction of his military leader, Othello, who did not promote him. Ultimately, Iago's web of deceit instigated the deaths of innocent victims, as well as his own death. Envy may be termed a wasted emotion, though we likely have all witnessed it, perhaps with social acquaintances, or between business competitors, or even among siblings. The criticism of another might be masking hidden resentment or envy. It is a trait of destruction and one to watch out for in ourselves.

It's never too late to change our negative qualities to positive ones. Daily self-study can show us where to be on guard, and meditation can deepen our desires for spiritual growth and heighten our awareness of God's goodness in all creation.

Gluttony is overindulgence in food or drink. This sin has resulted in personality, health, and financial problems for centuries, even in ancient times. The Old Testament states, "For the drunkard and the glutton will come to poverty" (Prov. 23:21).

Yet, though these sins are destructive, let us not condemn the glutton or drunkard, for we all have our own way of finding temporary escape from unhappiness. Release of pain and pressure comes in many forms. Some "work off" their anxiety by exercise, some lose themselves in drink, some gossip to vent their painful emotions, and some camouflage their escape by excessive sleep. Many of us overeat to find an external treat to compensate for our internal pain, as evidenced by today's high rate of obesity. While the food industry has done much to encourage unhealthy eating habits, we ourselves are ultimately responsible. Gluttony has become more and more accepted rather than faced as a sin. Yet sacred scripture faces the issue squarely: "Whose end is destruction, whose god is their belly, and whose glory is in their shame—who set their mind on earthly things" (Phil. 3:19). The harm of overindulgence is that we become enslaved by the body. Our passions rule us, whereas we should be ruling our habits. And because we live by habit, unhealthy and unproductive practices become hard to break.

Facing ourselves is the first step. Anyone with an addiction understands how it can dominate one's thinking. It certainly consumed mine. I hid my secret life from others and scheduled my days around meals. Just recently, self-honesty has begun to prevail. The overeating *can* be conquered. But for years I was unwilling to endure the needed self-discipline. I complained but did nothing about my problem. Why? The taste treat was too enticing, too hard to resist. How could I be happy without it? But food was a false satisfaction, for eating never satisfied the inner craving for spiritual fulfillment. I sought in the outer world that which can only be filled by the inner world of the soul.

This is not a judgment of anyone in a similar situation, for there are reasons for addictions. But the interior change of facing ourselves is the first step toward release from the mental and emotional anguish. As a recovering bulimic/anorexic, I can attest to these feelings. Though physicians and psychiatrists helped, the greatest progress came when I faced myself and began an honest daily self-evaluation of my desires and actions. When slips and failures came, I faced them squarely. And always, I turned to the Divine Physician for inner strength to fight my inner battle of the "eating monster"" that wanted more, and the "angel-of-right-reason" telling me no.

Directing our lives into positive paths takes hard work. Many would rather not make the effort. For the Master told us, "Enter by the narrow gate; for wide is the gate and broad is the way that leads to destruction, and there are many who go in by it. Because narrow is the gate and difficult is the way which leads to life, and there are few who find it" (Matt. 7:13–14). Practicing self-discipline is a narrow gate, but this path leads to a happier, higher existence. Perseverance takes hard work, but our slips into gluttony can be gradually overcome. The daily inventory provides a vehicle for discovering the *why* of our falls.

This information empowers us to avoid these pitfalls and to progress in conquering wrong habits.

Anger comes in various stages:
1. Facial expressions reveal irritation or annoyance.
2. Sharp words show resentment or offense.
3. Throwing or smashing things indicates exasperation, rage, and fury.
4. Anger, at its height, can desire the death of another, or commit the act.

These types of negative anger are not the righteous anger of the just man who feels moral indignation at wrongdoing, such as Jesus who overthrew the tables and chairs of the money changers and the dove merchants selling their wares in the temple area. Jesus spoke with authority, explaining that his father's house is to be a place of prayer and not a "den of thieves" (Mark 11:17). Jesus recognized the true motives of hypocrites who rejected him, while the seekers of Truth were drawn to his universal teachings.

Without desire to understand others, we may be blind to our own anger and intolerance toward those with different backgrounds. The person raised in surroundings of loud, immoral behavior is likely to manifest these same actions. And while abusive language may be the norm for some or the clothing of others not fit our expectations, we remember that the Master saw beyond a person's clothing or station in life. He provides a model for us and shows us that narrow-minded blame and judgment are not constructive. Rather, we need understanding of ourselves and awareness of others' points of view. Self-study can help us grow in this direction. One day, when teaching in high school, I was so frustrated at an uncooperative student that I threw chalk—and was astonished at myself! I'd just returned from the U.S. Army, where discipline and compliance with rules were routine. After twenty-two years of military service, I was out of touch with the changes in the civilian sector, and I "blew." Reflection on my unacceptable behavior showed me my lack of patience and understanding of the new generation. When anger or upset emotions prevail, it's time to reflect and search for the *why*.

Letting go of anger and releasing it is critical to mental and emotional health. Saint Paul tells us not to retire at night if we have been angry that day: "Do not let the sun go down on your wrath" (Eph. 4:26). Such advice prevents angry emotions from sinking into our hearts' cores, there to multiply and populate our secret thoughts. Rather, let us take the positive approach; that is, let go of emotional pain and let God fill us with Divine Love. This surrender to the Almighty's power to heal exemplifies the familiar saying, shown below.

Let go and let God.

Sloth shows itself in laziness, procrastination, listlessness, sluggishness, self-indulgence, and neglect of our duties. For example, we postpone the housecleaning or washing the car; we simply can't "get to" a difficult task; we don't keep to a schedule and are late for appointments, get up too late, or go to bed after midnight. We would rather enjoy our ease than do the moral or difficult things nagging at our conscience. Then, we blame others or excuse ourselves in order to justify our own failures. Facing sloth requires the willpower to actually do something about our failures. Failure itself is not necessarily a negative element; learning from our mistakes turns a painful lesson into a positive pathway. But we have to take the first step. Such a step may be taken by older adults pursuing a college degree who juggle important duties, such as making dinner for the family, holding a job, and doing homework. I've seen college students do this successfully, and often the family supports their efforts. At one time in my life, I held three jobs in order to repay a debt. The only way to do everything was to adhere to a strict schedule whether I felt like it or not—laundromat on Tuesday nights, waitressing other evenings, teaching preparations in the afternoons, housecleaning Saturday mornings. Mopping restaurant floors and carrying food trays was my exercise, and conversations with customers and students was my recreation. No time for TV or movies or weekend outings. Living within a budget and time schedule enabled me to repay the debt. I learned about not being slothful the hard way.

A daily schedule *can* be followed, finances *can* be disciplined, bad habits can be broken. Still, the hardest step may be acknowledging our behavior as sinful. For it's always easier to excuse ourselves than to discipline ourselves. One of the quickest ways to overcome sloth is to take small steps daily in the direction we wish to go. We may not be able to pay back a debt in full for a long time, but we can always manage to make small monthly payments; in this way we are moving forward and taking action on the problem. This principle can be applied to almost any endeavor. Learning to retire an hour earlier may be difficult, so back up bedtime fifteen minutes a week until the goal is reached. If cleaning the whole house is simply too much, clean a room each day instead. Indeed, Jesus himself spoke of laziness in the parable of the ten virgins. The bridegroom welcomed into the wedding feast the five virgins whose lighted lamps flashed a welcoming beacon upon his arrival, but the five virgins of slothful ways and darkened lamps wailed in sorrow as the wedding door shut against them.

Sloth can be internal or external; that is, we can be mentally lazy or physically lazy. Do we let our minds passively watch TV too much instead of energizing our minds by learning new things? Do we tell others to complete jobs we should finish? Do we ignore times of prayer, neglect to visit the sick, or not offer to help a friend? Sloth peeps through in unsuspecting ways. Limiting TV time was hard for me at first, but now I look forward to reading or taking an after-dinner walk or visiting a friend in the nursing home. Self-discipline brings a sense of freedom to do what we ought, not what we selfishly want. Also, dedicating a daily time for important projects helps set priorities in the day. For instance, while teaching college, this writer allocated a minimum of one hour daily to working on the manuscript for this book. Setting an amount of time daily for meditation, spiritual readings, and daily inventory helps to ensure these are fulfilled. Sometimes social events have had to wait or be curtailed in my life, but the importance of character growth was all-consuming. I was happier and a better person. I learned and grew in understanding without realizing it.

Self-study means looking in our own "cellars of sins." It's easy to rationalize our failures and bury them in excuses that pile up in our mental basement. It's easier to take our ease than turn the "should haves" into good deeds or duties well done. The undiscerning soul may not recognize the source of anxiety which stems from unfulfilled commitments.

But the Good Lord knows, for he seeks the sincere of heart, not the spiritually slothful. There is an old saying that actions speak louder than words. Rolling up our sleeves to sweep out our own sloth brightens the world around us and inspires others to follow.

4. **Daily Inventory Using Two Questions**
    Perhaps a basic way to get started on spiritual self-improvement is to ask two questions at the end of a day.
    a. Was I selfish today? Or was I kind today? When? How?
    b. Did I feel unhappy today? When? With whom?

Using these two questions, we apply them to four steps of reflection on our day:
   a.   We reflect on the hours gone by:
        Morning
        Lunch period
        Afternoon
        Dinner period
        Evening

   b.   If we discover selfishness or unhappiness at these times, we recall:
        Whom we were with
        Where we were
        When it was
        What the cause was (if we can't find this, we ask God's help)
        For example, if we felt irritated at a luncheon event, we think about those present, the food, the time of day, what was said. What actually triggered the irritation? *Why* did irritation come?

c.   The next step is determining what we can do to prevent the problem in the future. For example, in shopping lines we resolve to practice patience by sending goodwill to others or by saying the Lord's Prayer.

d.   And as a final step, we affirm taking this action. We *affirm* being patient in shopping lines, for example.

These, then, are four Daily Inventory methods:
Five Basic Needs
Development of Desirable Characteristics
Seven Cardinal Sins and Seven Cardinal Virtues
Two Questions
These tools offer an option for varying types of self-study. Each method sets before us a mirror of our daily behavior. The first method I used was the Five Basic Needs in order to gain awareness of my time use and to monitor health considerations. When these became routine, I shifted to observing my thinking and my motives. What an eye opener! For example, I discovered myself offering polite but insincere comments (for I failed to remember the reply). And I found myself being mentally critical or unkind when seeing certain people. Facing these faults has taken rigorous self-honesty—it's painful to face ourselves. Changing my old "mental grooves," as it were, into positive ones is not a quick process. It has required genuinely caring about others and realizing that we all come from different backgrounds. I don't know Sally's background or upbringing. I don't know Don's motives. How dare I assume so! How dare I judge another! For God is the final judge. We can rightly condemn the act of stealing but not condemn the one who steals. That action belongs to the Good God above and to the civil judge who acts to protect society. To judge another is failure to practice the Golden Rule, for we are all at varying stages of growth in every field. Because good can be found in everyone, we would do well to look for it rather than focus on our own narrow (and often arrogant) perspectives. Others' moral or ethical failures can be met with wishes for their healing and health. We should properly take the criminal out of society, but not send him cursing thoughts or despicable words, for such

behavior spews forth anger that breeds and multiplies. We should be instruments of creation, not destruction. Training ourselves to think this way requires thought *awareness* and a desire to lift society up, not tear it down.

Self-study aims at character perfection. Each stage of self-improvement brings the reward of renewed purpose. The old saying "success breeds success" has validity. Each forward step encourages us to take another. Let's get started on making ourselves better people. We become happier, and the world does too!

Chapter 3
Training Our Thoughts

Be transformed by the renewing of your mind.
Romans 12:2

In the small town where I live, a prominent sign in a health food store caught my eye. It read, "You are what you think about." These words show the source of our happiness and health. For how we think influences our total existence. We become what we think about.

From ancient times, sages have recognized this truth, recorded in sacred scripture:

"For as he thinks in his heart, so is he" (Prov. 23:7). If we think about something deeply, we eventually become it.

"A sound heart is life to the body, but envy is rottenness to the bones" (Prov. 14:30). Righteous thoughts create a sound heart, free of guilt, free to love.

"Hear, O earth! Behold, I will certainly bring calamity on this people—the fruit of their thoughts, because they have not heeded My words nor My law, but rejected it" (Jer. 6:19). Think evil toward another, and evil joins itself to you.

"For from within, out of the hearts of men, proceed evil thoughts, adulteries, fornications, murders, thefts, covetousness, wickedness, deceit, lewdness, an evil eye, blasphemy, pride, foolishness. All these evils things come from within and defile a man" (Mark 7:21–23).

Saint Paul tells us to "be transformed by the renewing of [our] mind" (Rom. 12:2). Our actions start in the mind—in our thoughts.

In other words, what we think about affects our existence, moment by moment. If we feel at a loss or depressed, finding renewed hope wipes away the anguish. Our thinking process has changed from negative to positive. New energy surges up from within. Consider the ancient Hebrews enslaved for four hundred years in Egypt— depressed and discouraged. Moses appeared and brought new hope; the worn, torn Israelites rallied and followed him through the desert to the Promised Land, albeit not without difficulty. When their thoughts were positive, strong action followed.

The importance of our thought life is highlighted most emphatically by the Ten Commandments. We are told to love the Lord our God with all our mind and not to covet (or ardently desire for) our neighbor's wife nor any of his possessions. (Exod. 20: 1–17). Thousands of years later, Jesus the Master built upon this concept in the Sermon on The Mount when telling his listeners that whoever looks at a woman and lusts after her (covets her with his thoughts) has already committed adultery with her in his heart. (Matt. 5:27–28) Our Lord focuses on sin at its source—in the mind. And Bishop Sheen in more recent times continues the theme: "When one meditates and fills his mind for an hour a day with thoughts and resolutions bearing on the love of God and neighbor above all things, there is a gradual seepage of love down to the level of what is called the subconscious, and finally these good thoughts emerge, of themselves, in the form of effortless good actions."[19] So let us watch our thoughts and keep them pure and kindly in nature. We will make ourselves, and others, happier as a result.

Our emotion-thoughts often conflict with our reason-thoughts. We don't relish getting out of bed on a frosty morning, but rational thought reminds us not to be late for work. We may not like a particular task in the day, but reason prevails and we do our duty. However, if emotion-thoughts dominate, we become victims of our moods or bad habits, and we spiral downward in behavior and attitude. On the other hand, rational thought curbs the imbalanced emotional swings, enabling us to lead productive lives and contribute to the world. The tussle between our reason and passions, between our spirit and our senses, goes on continuously, and unless we are vigilant, imbalanced emotion can overwhelm our lives, leaving us distressed and wondering, "How did I ever get this way?"

The key is to harness our thoughts and keep them on paths of goodness. When a temptation comes, mentally reject it. Then replace the temptation with its opposite. If the temptation is toward immorality, turn your eyes away from the tempting picture, screen, or person. Instead, look at other things and identify with purity of thought. If the temptation is toward buying an unneeded item, practice contentment with what you have. Unless we control our thoughts, our imbalanced thoughts and desires can control us. So let's harness our thoughts and train them to be positive forces in our lives.

There is an old saying: "Thoughts are things." We can't touch or see thoughts, but they are real. Though we can't touch or see the wind, we nonetheless see its effects, evident in branches swaying in the breeze and clouds sweeping across the heavens. Sound waves are not visible to the naked eye, but sand atop a music player will move in designs dictated by the sound vibrations. In the same way, invisible thoughts betray themselves in a facial expression or tapping pencil. Thoughts of stealing, if dwelled upon, can lead to a theft. Impure thoughts, dwelled upon, can produce impure actions. We develop our thinking habits based on how often and how intensely we think something. As Bishop Sheen accurately claimed, though we would not allow garbage to be served at the dinner table, we often allow it to be served into our thoughts via impure and violent media technologies.[20]

We rarely ponder the importance of our thought lives, and unfortunately, leave our imaginations free to wander. People who may not meet our approval in speech or personal appearance tend to spark our wordless disapproval and less-than-kind thoughts. Unknowingly, we have just caused ourselves unpleasant emotions and sent them to another—based on the thoughts we allowed into our minds. Why do we feel repelled by the presence of some people and cheered by the presence of others? Because inaudible thoughts emanate from us all, and we intuitively recognize the "good or bad vibes" of others, as it were. Have you ever simply disliked someone for no rational reason? Or, on the other hand, felt a kinship with a new acquaintance? Notice how a baby may unhappily squirm in rejection of some people but coo in the arms of others.

In *The Power of Positive Thinking*, Dr. Norman V. Peale tells an interesting story of looking out of a train window one day as the train waited in the station. Dr. Peale saw a small boy sitting on the curb, and he sent kindly thoughts toward the lad. Suddenly, the boy looked up and smiled in return.[21] Our thoughts are a form of prayer.

To counteract any of our own negative thought patterns, we can consciously train ourselves to think in positive ways. The first step is becoming aware of our thoughts day in and day out. We all know people who continually tend to find something wrong with people, with an organization, or with the government. Their "joy" seems to be tearing down people and systems. And being around such people casts a cloud over our sunny dispositions. Conversely, we all know people who have a smile on their face and a kind word for all. And our spirits are lifted just by being in their presence. Why not select a day to consciously be aware of our own thoughts? Do we tend to be negative or optimistic? Are we automatically tense around certain people? Do we face each day with a routine set of fears? Are we eager to get up in the morning and greet the day? If not, why not? Whatever our thoughts are, we broadcast them to ourselves, to the people we meet, and even to our pets. Becoming aware of our thoughts is the first step in thought training.

The next step is repeating positive statements throughout the day to create within ourselves a spirit of optimism, of courage, and of good cheer toward others. We find ourselves empowered with a pleasant spirit of perseverance and fortitude and a desire to get the job done. Result? We meet obstacles with resiliency and recognize failures as vehicles for self-study. Those honest with themselves can recognize a deficient method or perhaps an unworthy motive. Ultimately, new joy in life emerges as we grow stronger in strengthening our character.

What are the "positive words" we should repeat to ourselves? Many people enjoy repeating biblical verses (or parts of them) throughout the day or saying a short prayer before starting the car. Some people carry the verses in their purses or wallets to read in the doctor's waiting room or prior to an exam. I know a woman who carries a pocket edition of the New Testament in her purse. One day, while she was reading it in a hospital waiting room, a young man next to her asked if she would look up a verse in James, and they had an interesting discussion. He'd turned from any church at that point in his life, but he was still interested in finding God. Another method of keeping positive thoughts is to repeat the Lord's Prayer when in a slow cashier line or, if anger descends, to remember, "Anger is mine, sayeth the Lord" (Deut. 32:35, paraphrased). Long ago, Saint Paul urged the early Christians to "Rejoice always" (1 Thess. 5:16). Impossible? Not if our hearts and minds have been trained to be continually turned Above in attitude and thought.

Our thoughts create our states of mind. Thinking evil thoughts is like hanging out a sign in the Unseen World that attracts other negative/evil energies, according to English physician, psychiatrist, and scientist Dr. Alexander Cannon: "Did not Paul say, 'We wrestle not against flesh and blood, but against principalities, against powers, against the rulers of the darkness of this world' (Eph. 6:12)?"[22] That is, we wrestle with the mental world of man as surely as we do the physical world. Why do we shield our children from horror movies or violence on TV? Horror images stimulate horror thoughts, and young ones can remain terrified, though snuggled under warm blankets. Children may develop nightmares and fear "bad people" under their beds.

On the other hand, thinking positive thoughts stimulates positive results. One day at the check-out counter of the local discount store, I fell into conversation with the cashier who had to walk home in the dark. I expressed to her my belief that she could draw about herself unseen forces of good by her thoughts of God's power and love. I've employed this concept myself when walking home from the library after dark. The store clerk seemed uplifted to realize that her own thoughts of God's goodness can draw his angelic protection around us.

And it truly does. Years ago, a young woman in the Salvation Army walked unharmed through the lowest economic strata of a large city, seeking out society's castaways. The drunkards and derelicts never touched her, for they would not violate Goodness, as it compassionately walked in their midst and bound their wounds.[23] Our minds are like magnets. Our pure thoughts bring Unseen Protection and draw out the hidden reserves of goodness in every soul. Conversely, our evil thoughts will attract others of the same tendency.

Jesus recognized the intentions of others—the earnestness of true seekers and the hypocrisy of others. Those of good intentions were attracted to him, and those as yet unwilling to face their selfishness rejected him. The old saying "Birds of a feather flock together" has a psychological basis. Pure souls are not comfortable among impure people, and vice versa, for a lack of kindred spirit exists.

Using the analogy of our mind as a wireless radio or television receiver, we can turn the dial of our attention to any station we wish in the Unseen World of ether, where thought waves ceaselessly circulate. God continually sends out broadcasts of love, goodness, and justice. By keeping our mental antennae tuned to His station, we become receptive to positive, uplifting energies and can meet obstacles with fortitude. We respond with compassion toward those on the wrong path. Yet, if we allow our thoughts to spin uncontrollably, or if we are not in charge of our mind's frequency dial, we may become subject to unkind and evil forces also sending forth their powerful mental vibrations. The choice is ours. Where we put our attention, our thoughts follow, and our thoughts produce our future.

Hence, most religions have taught the importance of continual prayer, continued awareness of God's Laws, and strong moral/ethical conduct to sustain lasting harmony in the universe. "God is love," state the scriptures (1 John 4:8). Love does not destroy; love creates and builds up. To be channels for harmony and love, we would do well to remember the words of Saint Paul: "Pray without ceasing" (1 Thess. 5:17). Our continued good thoughts are a form of "praying without ceasing." The ancient Hebrews were directed by Moses to remember the Laws of God in their hearts and in their thoughts: "You shall teach them [the words of the Law] diligently to your children, and shall talk of them when you sit in your house, when you walk by the way, when you lie down, and when you rise up. You shall bind them as a sign on your hand, and they shall be as frontlets between your eyes. You shall write them on the doorposts of your house and on your gates" (Deut. 6:6–9).

This directive reflects the psychological truth that repetition sears words into the thought processes of our mind. Medical students review names of bones over and over, and language students recite their vocabulary lessons. In the same way, our spiritual lessons need repetition. These reminders abound in all religions—symbols people wear and place in their homes, important annual religious ceremonies, and traditions that provide reinforcement to the faith. Thus an important key to our physical and mental health is keeping our daily thoughts turned toward universal forces of good. Anyone in the pit of addictive behavior knows the extreme difficulty of lifting the mind Above during an addiction attack. One preventive tactic may be to avoid the environment of the addictive behavior. The alcoholic consciously avoids streets with bars and lounges. The lustful avoid sensual images. Because the bulimic must eat to live, she develops tactics of self-control, such as not eating between meals and practicing good manners at the table. And the spiritual aspirant can dine as though with the Divine Guest. Such efforts require real discipline, for entrenched habits can be hard to change.

Today's science now supports this concept. Medical professionals recognize that the cells of our body contain intelligence and can be likened to little nations, which respond to thoughts of cheer and comfort, just as we do.[24] Imagine our cells as survivors of an earthquake buried under wreckage with limited oxygen. If we call to the survivor that rescue efforts will take two hours, and the oxygen is quickly going, depression or panic could easily seize the victim. But if we call down words of encouragement, the survivor's hope can help him hang on. Our cells have only our thoughts to inspire them, and constructive thoughts help stimulate an optimal secretion of hormones into our bloodstreams, resulting in an upswing in emotional and physical health. Thus, the more we hold on to positive attitudes, the greater the hormonal homeostasis of our body. Better mind-body health is the inevitable result.

The term psychosomatic illness comes from the recognition that there is a mind-body (psyche-soma) relationship. Having morbid thoughts of fear of the local flu bug can help bring on the illness in us. Medically documented mind-body illnesses reveal that negative thoughts stimulate our brains (namely, the pituitary gland) to initiate hormone secretions in other parts of our body. For example, if we face a charging bear, thoughts of fear produce increased adrenaline from the adrenal glands to help us respond quickly. But continued negative thoughts produce a continued stream of hormones in our body, producing an *imbalance* in the circulatory system.[25]

The continual stress of many lifestyles today can eventually produce illness, resulting from prolonged hormonal imbalance. We witness the heart attacks of high-level executives with a pattern of worry or anger in reaction to business turmoil. But stress in the form of loneliness can also contribute to health problems. Thus, more and more western medical practitioners are treating the psychological as well as physical condition.[26]

Hence, we can help improve our own health by training our thoughts to flow in positive channels. By our own efforts, we can help stem the tide of negative or destructive emotions that stunt our growth in every way. When a rainy morning or a flat tire mar our day, we would do well to see these as opportunities to change irritation into optimism and to convert frustration into perseverance. The wisdom of Solomon still advises us: "A merry heart does good, like medicine, but a broken spirit dries the bones" (Prov. 17:22).

We see the validity of these words whenever we are happily engaged in productive work. Anyone consumed by a passion for his work finds that time disappears. Become eager in our work, and the preoccupation with an addiction or a worry vanishes.

The power of thought operates in the spiritual realm as well, explained by Our Lord in numerous ways. In the Sermon on the Mount, he stated the Universal Law of cause and effect—that what we give (in our thoughts and deeds), we will receive: "For with what judgment you judge, you will be judged; and with the measure you use, it will be measured back to you" (Matt. 7:2). In other words, give goodwill, and goodwill returns. Cheat another, and that also will return.

By concentrating on the material world and ignoring the spiritual laws, we become negative, grasping, and fearful, a result of undue emphasis on worldly wishes. And since the basis of our outlook is our thoughts, the basis of our health is the same. Send out loving, compassionate thoughts, and they will be returned by others. The positive emotions generated in this way uplift both the sender and receiver. Conversely, if we send out hateful, jealous thoughts, people will turn away, for they pick up our thoughts quite intuitively. People may be unaware why they feel repelled by certain people—studying their thoughts would be revealing.

There is an unconscious turning away from someone who is arrogant or selfish. Children and animals innately recognize the kindly or the angry nature of a visitor. The toddler smiles or shies away; the horse takes the sugar or nips your hand. But as thinking adults, we can become instruments for good in the face of selfishness. If we are targets of spiteful words from another, we can break the circle of negative feelings by offering a calm response. Our calmness disarms the angry soul; his dart drops to the floor. The transformation of a relationship has begun. The importance of our thought-world is mirrored in scripture's sound psychological advice: "A wrathful man stirs up strife, but he who is slow to anger allays contention" (Prov. 15:18). But we cannot control our words without developing awareness of our thoughts.

To become consciously aware of our responses, mentally or verbally, let's consider the psychologist's classic models of reactions to an obstacle. The obstacle could be physical, such as being in a traffic jam or without money. The obstacle could be emotional, such as anger at promotion failure or despair at a loved one's death. Three traditional responses to meeting obstacles are aggression, retreat, or a solution based on balanced reason.

- The aggressive person smashes through the obstacle: he steals, punches, yells. His behavior reveals unruly emotions rather than use of reason and stable thoughts.

- The person who retreats may become silent and withdrawn, sometimes fearful of doing otherwise. But sometimes retreat is appropriate, exemplified by the general who temporarily retreats in battle due to overwhelming odds, but later advances to victory. There is a true story of a newly married couple who had a heated argument. She began smashing the dishes. In response, he got in the car and went for a drive. When both were calm, they discussed the matter rationally and found the source of misunderstanding. The husband's retreat was temporary and consciously chosen, for he realized this was the best avenue to mutual understanding and reconciliation. On the other hand, retreating continuously, through fear, may merely push the painful emotions farther down into our subconscious, only to manifest in subsequent unhealthy ways. Sudden rage may erupt following a period of submerged anger.

- The person who seeks a universal and balanced solution to a problem goes around the obstacle to achieve a goal. For example, instead of cheating in school, the sincere person studies and learns the material. The truthful person earns his way honestly.

Thus by learning to be aware of our thoughts, we learn to assess our reactions in daily life. Do we respond with improper aggression, with fearful retreat, or with a reasoned solution? Do we respond to arguments by shouting back at others rather than sitting down and discussing problems logically? Or are emotions too strong, making it necessary for a mediator to intervene? Do we eat or drink too much without analyzing why? Do we spend too much money?

Awareness of our thoughts, on the surface and down deep, is critical to our mental, emotional, and spiritual evolution.

- Emotionally, we become calmer, more patient.

- Psychologically, we apply reason (1) to seek self-understanding and (2) to pinpoint sources of anxiety in our daily life.

- Spiritually, we release tension by meditation and find renewed insight to solve problems.

The key to a universal response to our problems is to find detachment from them. Then a reasoned solution can emerge. To accomplish this end, we change the direction of our thoughts by meditation; we turn *from* the outer material world *to* the inner spiritual world. That is, we change the polarity of our minds. For example, instead of worrying about a promotion, we meditate on God as reflected in spiritual qualities, such as compassion, truthfulness, righteousness. Instead of *dwelling on* our worldly anxieties, we *release* them by *turning* our thoughts in a spiritual direction. Then the "answers" from God can flow to us. Imagine a fist closed tightly around a problem or a worry. God's peace cannot pour in, for the fist is closed tightly around the worry. But when the fist is opened, the worry can drift away and God's peace can enter. Our minds are then receptive to God's solution. Our thoughts can then operate on a higher level. As we "let go" of worries, we "let God" show us the way. When our thoughts focus on giving rather than getting, we change.

Becoming aware of our thoughts daily helps lift us to a more loving and righteous level of living. If someone is late to a meeting, rather than mentally condemning the person, we realize that we do not know the reason for his or her tardiness. There may be a valid reason; we do not judge. If a young mother in the grocery line has a dirty, squalling youngster in tow, rather than condemning the mother, we send her wishes of peace and healing of tensions in her life.

It is as if each of us moves through life enclosed in the circular, transparent dome through which we see all of life, shaded by our own upbringings and circumstances. Each of us sees life through the window of our own past. Because of this, our responses to life are not, and cannot be, the same as others' responses. Hence, it's easy to judge and misunderstand our neighbors, for we do not see life as they do. Late arrival for meetings may not bother some; it may irritate others. Judgment assigns blame, and blame is not a constructive force. Rather, we need understanding and an objective, compassionate response to life. Because each person responds to life differently, each of us sees life from our own, individual perspectives.

We respond to life through our own glass, as do others. No need to judge if we see wrongs. Instead, we should remain objective and recognize true injustice for what it is. We recognize poor manners for what they are, but never judge, for we have not lived another's life. To become instruments of "good," we become examples of honest behavior and courteous words. By a life of good example, we help lift the world around us.

Chapter 4
Universal Application

Universal Law applies to all people in every country and every century.

For example, an everyday saying, such as "What goes around, comes around" reflects a cyclical natural law. And it is also recorded scripture:

"And behold, I am coming quickly, and My reward is with Me, to give to every one according to his work" (Rev. 22:12).

"I, the Lord, search the heart, I test the mind, even to give every man according to his ways, according to the fruit of his doings" (Jer. 17:10).

As we give, so shall we receive. If we send out unkind thoughts; unkindness will come back to us. When we return a lost wallet, our losses will be replaced. Natural law operates on the human level and in the spiritual realm as well. There was a man who wanted to sell his car's seat covers to make some money, but sudden inspiration prompted him to give them to a poor person with an old vehicle. That same day, the man received a free set of damaged but still highly usable seat covers for his new car. The spiritual law manifested itself in a single day. This same-day witness of the Universal Law, however, is often not the case, and thus we may be slow to realize that good things in our lives stem from earlier kindnesses to others.

Other natural or universal laws also exist, such as the duality in the universe (day/night or hot/cold, for example) and the relationship of mind and body (psychosomatic illness). Such truths can be expressed by both the philosophical person and the scientist. The scientist discovers truths from the outside—via scientific observation. We read of scientific experiments revealing new knowledge, such as unlocking the secrets of DNA. In the psychological realm, Sigmund Freud discovered new sources of human behavior through psychoanalysis. Recent science shows how the "brain space" of one habit can be replaced by a different habit. In Dr. Norman Doidge's *The Brain That Changes Itself*, we read that people can continue to learn well into adulthood. Thus, an old dog can learn new tricks. During babyhood, Dr. Doidge continues, our brains are very plastic (that is, can adapt to changes), thus explaining why languages are easier for us to learn as children. But today's science shows the why of the saying "use it or lose it," referring to a skill or habit. Brain images can now be visually reproduced and studied. They show how repeated activities (piano practice, for example) take dominance inside the brain map. When the piano student fails to practice his lessons, not only is piano-playing skill diminished, but the "piano space" in the brain map is taken over by other activities the person is doing. This new science could explain why repeated unwanted habits are hard to break. The brain space of the *unwanted* habit has to be replaced by a countering good activity.[27] Thus the duality of universe, the opposites of good and evil for example, might be reflected in the concrete world of our brain matter. That is, identify with honesty, and its opposite, stealing, might be eliminated. Thus we can recognize the importance of our thinking. Giving time and attention to righteous practices can replace the unrighteous ones.

While the scientist discovers truths from the outside, the spiritually centered soul discovers truths from the inside—via a godly mind and heart developed through prayer and meditation. We read that King Solomon's phenomenal wisdom resulted from deep communion with God. We read of sages with inexplicable insight who never learned to read. Whence comes this knowledge, if not from Above?

Turning the mind from the outside world of matter to the inside world of mind is called meditation by some, while others call it mental relaxation. Either phrase turns the mind away from the magnetism of the outside world of matter and toward the magnetism of the inside world of spirit, where we release tensions, think more clearly, and receive new ideas—answers to prayer and to questions.

Living a universal balanced life involves balancing our individual desires with desires for the good of all. The selfish person does not care if the radio blares and disturbs a neighbor. But the balanced person recognizes the right of others to their peace and quiet and turns down the music or uses earphones. The selfish person lies and cheats to get ahead and eventually pays for this deceit by a guilt-ridden conscience, poor health, and, someday, somewhere, loss of ill-gotten gain. On the other hand, the balanced person who acts righteously may take time to succeed, but his heart is free of guilt, which elicits a natural cheerfulness and contributes to a healthy constitution.

Both the spiritual and scientific approaches to life may include a daily life of meditation (or mental relaxation), of self-study (the daily inventory), and of thought training to keep our minds on higher, righteous goals.

Both the scientific and spiritual approach recognize a Ruling Force in the universe. The scientist acknowledges the natural laws governing the universe, such as gravity or the cycle of seasons. The person who is spiritually centered recognizes God's laws as the source of harmony to people and governments. Violation of these laws produces disharmony and destruction. History records it. Violation of the Golden Rule has resulted in numerous wars. But this situation does not have to exist. Pope Paul II sought to bridge the intolerance gap by meeting with youth around the world and by meeting with leaders of other faiths. Family feuds can harm children and grandchildren. Even Shakespeare's *Romeo and Juliet* is an example of lovers who inherited a family feud and died as a result.

But in order to have a world that creates rather than destroys, one requirement exists for both the scientist and the philosopher. That requirement is honoring the Golden Rule and codes of moral, ethical conduct in life. For these produce harmonious relationships between peoples, cultures, and nations. Conversely, self-centeredness and unrighteous motives bring about disharmony and destruction— between individuals and nations.

People need to be able to depend on something that is real. The world changes, but true order does not. Universal values and principles do not change. The Ten Commandments are as valid today as ever.

Any deviation from moral, ethical living destroys, brings chaos—to the individual, to friendships, to families, to governments, to world peace. Scientific knowledge is helpful only if it is used to benefit mankind in the *long* run. People need a guiding principle by which to order their lives. The Seven Cardinal Virtues are such a standard.

The Seven Cardinal Virtues

Faith
Fortitude
Patience
Perseverance
Humility
Justice
Temperance
Also: Charity, Spirituality/Chastity

Love encompasses them all—love of the Good of the Whole more than of the personal self. Man-made systems are subject to error. Only God's Laws are trustworthy. Incorporating these into our daily lives brings inward peace and outward goodwill.

Everyone can benefit:
1. By meditating upon God to release tension and find inner peace
2. By doing a daily inventory to improve character
3. By training one's thoughts to focus on constructive goals which help mankind

Everyone's life is bound to improve following these steps.

The quickest way to progress personally is to follow the Divine Master who modeled what He taught. Jesus of Nazareth, while being nailed to the cross, said, "Forgive them Father, for they know not what they do." Thus we are to forgive our enemies, but not give in to their rejection of the true. Jesus of Nazareth led by personal example. Before asking his disciples to offer their lives in service of mankind, he did so himself and personally washed the feet of his own disciples, saying, "For I have given you an example" (John 13:15). But the effort to follow the Master must be wholehearted, not followed only when convenient to our plans or preferences. In the same way a parent must rechannel a recalcitrant, disobedient child into right paths, the Good Lord must administer medicine to his wayward children on earth who refuse to follow his laws—laid down for their health and harmony of soul.

Jesus of Nazareth came to raise the consciousness of those willing to practice the Golden Rule in its highest sense. Jesus the Master told us to be merciful (Matt. 5:7), that is, to recognize the hurts of others. The merciful soul can rise above petty grievances and genuinely care about another, as did the Good Samaritan who helped another in need. The merciful heart remembers that all of us are souls, just like he is. In respect of each as a soul, he treats all justly, kindly, correctly. Moreover, he gives personal time to self-understanding (daily inventory), to communing with Divinity (meditation), and to directing his thoughts into constructive channels (thought training). The message of Jesus still speaks to us, for Divine Truth never goes out of date.

In Palestine over two thousand years ago, those unwilling to face their arrogance, deceit, and greed refused to listen to the Master, and they still do today. Yet, the Savior's message of righteous living still rings true. The more we justify unkind words, white lies, and deceitful intention, the more we practice self-deceit—and reap the consequences: unhappiness. Self-honesty is the key to reversal of frustration. How? By changing our life's purpose from seeking the lower mansions of materialism to seeking the higher mansions of the soul: character perfection. Biblical truths offer the highest wisdom of universal living, if we apply them personally—actually do it.

Those unwilling to make the effort tread water rather than swim forward and miss the joy of self-growth. Mental or physical pain is a signal for us that we are on the wrong path. We can find the right path by analyzing our situation and facing our true motives. Freedom from the bondage of worldly attachments takes work. Thus, Jesus let us know that the narrow (disciplined) path leads to the higher life. But many would rather follow the wide (easy) path, and thus they treasure bigger, physical mansions rather than *higher* mansions of the *soul*.

> *In My Father's house are many mansions;*
> *If it were not so, I would have told you.*
> *I go to prepare a place for you.*
> John 14:2

The more we discipline our thoughts and actions to pursue righteous paths, the happier and healthier we become. Jesus shows us this path in the two Great Commandments of loving God and loving neighbor.

The Two Great Commandments of Jesus
You shall love the Lord your God with all your heart,
with all your soul, and with all your mind.
This is the first and great commandment.
And the second is like it:
You shall love your neighbor as yourself.
On these two commandments
hang all the Law and the Prophets.
Matthew 22:37–40

To act upon Jesus's commands, we use a three-pronged blueprint for balanced self-improvement, leading to *limitless self-perfection* in our eternal existence.

1. We meditate on God.
We trust the spirit to:
- remove painful emotions

- bring peace of soul

- guide our steps in positive paths

2. We conduct a daily inventory.
We measure our thoughts and behavior against the unchanging Principles of Righteousness.
- Are we measuring up to the Seven Cardinal Virtues? Are the Seven Cardinal Sins a stumbling block?

- How do we measure up to the Ten Commandments lived out in our daily lives (Exod. 20:2–17)?

- Are we examples of constant Christianity, as reflected in the Sermon on the Mount (Matt. 5–7)?

3. We train our thoughts.
In heart and mind, we honor right living.
Why? To help bring about:
- A righteous world

- A harmonious neighborhood

- A loving family

Constant Christianity is the never-ending climb up the Mountain of God. The circular climb upward is natural and within God's cycles: the daily cycle of the sun's rising and setting; the yearly cycle of the earth's rotation of the sun; the annual cycle of the four seasons' rebirth of nature; and our cycles of personal growth during the upward climb to God.

Jesus gave us a parable for encouragement. Unless a grain of wheat falls to the earth and sheds its outer shell, new life will not spring forth (John 12:24). In like manner, each of us must shed our outer shells of selfishness in order to bring forth new spiritual lives of the mind. "Be transformed by the renewing of your mind," urges Saint Paul (Rom. 12:2).

This daily process of renewal starts with meditation, which lifts our minds to higher vistas, sweeps out the pain, and fills us with vigor and enthusiasm for the day. Then we arise with optimism, and throughout the day we train ourselves to banish negative (hurtful) thoughts and replace them with righteous motives and deeds. At day's end, we reflect on our spiritual progress, using eternal virtues as our guide and measuring stick.

Our trials during the upward climb, though difficult, need not be overwhelming, for the Good Lord's sustaining words echo in our heart: "Lo, I am with you always, even to the end of the age" (Matt. 28:20).

Trials can be turned into opportunities for growth. But growth is painful, as any tiny child can tell us. It hurts to fall down when developing new muscles for walking. Building new character muscles may also be painful—as we give effort but miss the mark. Yet the tiny child perseveres, innately driven to become fully human. So we, too, must persevere to develop the skills of a virtuous life.

Truly, the pursuit of constant Christianity blossoms into the beauty of sterling character and a happy, productive life.

*Therefore you shall be **perfect**, just as your Father in heaven is perfect.*
(Matt. 5:48).

*The Lord will **perfect** that which concerns me.*
(Ps. 138:8)

Notes

1. Benson, *The Relation Response*, 67.
2. Ibid., 62.
3. Hewett, *Conceptual Physics*, 720.
4. Dawson, *The Basic Teachings*, 6.
5. Sheen, *Lift up Your Heart*, 201.
6. Ibid., 200.
7. Art History Guide.
8. "The Joy of Meditation," 19.
9. Oz, *Healing from the Heart*, 156.
10. Siegel, *Love, Medicine & Miracles*, 37.
11. Ibid., 49.
12. Schindler, *How to Live*, 59.
13. Pernoud, *The Retrial of Joan of Arc*, 179.
14. Dickens, *A Christmas Carol*, 39.
15. Begbie, *Broken Earthenware*, 43.
16. Franklin, "The Autobiography," 78–88.
17. Graham, *Freedom from the Seven Deadly Sins*, introduction.
18. Sheen, *Lift up Your Heart*, 19.
19. Ibid., 204.
20. Ibid., 115.
21. Peale, *The Power of Positive Thinking*, 60.
22. Cannon, *Powers That Be*, 40.
23. Begbie, *Broken Earthenware*, 28.
24. Cannon, *Powers That Be*, 30.
25. Benson, *The Relation Response*, 17-19.
26. Siegel, *Love, Medicine & Miracles*, 180.
27. Doidge, *The Brain That Changes Itself*, 46–61.

Bibliography

Art History Guide. "Grandma Moses Biography." http://www.
  arthistoryguide.com/travel/travel29.aspx

Begbie, Harold. *Broken Earthenware*. London: Hodder & Stoughton
  Ltd., 1965.

Benson, Herbert. *The Relation Response*. New York: William Morrow
  & Co., Inc. 1975.

Blanton, Smiley, M.D. *Love or Perish*. New York: Simon and Schuster,
  1956.

Cannon, Alexander, M.D. *Powers That Be*. New York: Dutton,
  1968.

————. *The Power Within*. New York: Dutton, 1960.

Dawson, Miles Menander. *The Basic Teachings of Confucius*. New
  York: New Home Library, 1942.

Dickens, Charles. *A Christmas Carol*. New York: Dover Thrift
  Editions, 1991.

Doidge, Norman, M.D. *The Brain That Changes Itself*. New York:
  Penguin, 2007.

Franklin, Benjamin. "The Autobiography of Benjamin Franklin," ed.
  Charles W. Eliot. *Harvard Classics, The Five Foot Shelf of Books,
  Volume 1*. New York: Collier & Sons, 1909.

Gibran, Kahlil. *The Prophet*. New York: Alfred A. Knopf, 1973.

Graham, Billy. *Freedom from The Seven Deadly Sins*. Zondervan
  Publishing House: Grand Rapids, 1967.

Hewett, Paul G. *Conceptual Physics*, eighth ed., Reading, MA:
  Addison-Wesley, 1998.

"The Joy of Meditation," *Positive Thinking Magazine*. New York:
  Guideposts, Sept/Oct. 2005, p. 19.

Leadbeater, C.W. *The Chakras*. Wheaton, IL: Theosophical, 1972.

————. *Man Visible and Invisible*. Wheaton, IL: Theosophical, 1975.

New American Bible, St. Joseph Edition. New York: Catholic Publishing Corp., 1992.

Oz, Mehmet, M.D. *Healing from the Heart*. New York: Plume, 1999.

Peale, Norman Vincent. *The Power of Positive Thinking*. New York: Fawcett Crest, 1990.

Pernoud, Regine. *The Retrial of Joan of Arc; the Evidence for Her Vindication*. Transl. Cohen, J.M. San Francisco: Ignatius Press, 2007.

Schindler, John A., M.D. *How to* Live *365 Days a Year*. Greenwich: Fawcett Crest, 1954.

Sheen, Fulton J. *Lift up Your Heart: A Guide to Spiritual Peace*. Liguori, MO: Liguori/Triumph, 1997.

Siegel, Bernie S., M.D. *Love, Medicine & Miracles*. New York: Perennial, 1988.